MW01618300

R. J. Rushdoony

In His Service

The Christian Calling to Charity

Vallecito, California

In His Service:
The Christian Calling to Charity
by R.J. Rushdoony)
(published posthumously)

Ross House Books
PO Box158
Vallecito, CA 95251
www.ChalcedonStore.com

Library of Congress: 2009921211
ISBN: 978-1-879998-54-48

Other titles by
Rousas John Rushdoony

The Institutes of Biblical Law, Vol. I
The Institutes of Biblical Law, Vol. II, Law & Society
The Institutes of Biblical Law, Vol. III, The Intent of the Law
Systematic Theology (2 volumes)
Commentaries on the Pentateuch: Genesis, Exodus, Leviticus, Numbers, Deuteronomy
Chariots of Prophetic Fire
Sermon on the Mount
The Gospel of John
Romans & Galatians
Hebrews, James, & Jude
The Cure of Souls
Sovereignty
The Death of Meaning
Noble Savages
Larceny in the Heart
To Be As God
The Biblical Philosophy of History
The Mythology of Science
Thy Kingdom Come
Foundations of Social Order
This Independent Republic
The Nature of the American System
The "Atheism" of the Early Church
The Messianic Character of American Education
The Philosophy of the Christian Curriculum
Christianity and the State
Salvation and Godly Rule
God's Plan for Victory
Politics of Guilt and Pity
Roots of Reconstruction
The One and the Many
Revolt Against Maturity
By What Standard?
Law & Liberty

Chalcedon
PO Box 158 * Vallecito, CA 95251
www.ChalcedonStore.com

This publication was made possible
thanks to the generosity
of the families of
Christ Church in Branchville, Alabama

Contents

ONE

The Place of Biblical Law in Society

To ask about the place of Biblical law in society can be compared to asking about the place of sun and oxygen in our material life. Such a comparison only dimly approximates the necessity for God's revealed law in our social order.

The Westminster Shorter Catechism, number 14, tells us, "Sin is any want of conformity unto, or transgression of, the law of God." This echoes 1 John 3:4, "Whosoever committeth sin transgresseth also the law: for sin is the transgression of the law." We are also told:

> But he that sinneth against me wrongeth his own soul: all they that hate me love death. (Prov. 8:36)

> For the wages of sin is death; but the gift of God is eternal life through Christ Jesus our Lord. (Rom. 6:23)

Paul also tell us:

> 8. For by grace are ye saved through faith; and that not of yourselves: it is the gift of God:
> 9. Not of works, lest any man should boast.

> 10. For we are his workmanship, created in Christ Jesus unto good works, which God hath before ordained that we should walk in them. (Eph. 2:8–10)

We are saved by God's sovereign grace through faith, and we have not been saved to despise His law, His justice or righteousness. Rather, Paul says, God beforehand prepared us and ordained our regeneration: He "created [us] in Christ Jesus for good works." We crucify Christ afresh when we despise His law.

In Scripture, the word justice is the same in meaning as righteousness. Justice or righteousness is moral order and is a religious fact. Laws express views of justice or moral order and are thus an establishment of religion. Laws do not per se establish a church but rather a religion, and necessarily so. Hence, the only kind of law acceptable from a Biblical perspective is God's law: "Except the LORD build the house, they labour in vain that build it" (Ps. 127:1).

How does the Lord build His House or Kingdom? We have too long sought to establish God's law order through the state or the church. Both are necessary but *limited* spheres under God. Scripture specifically limits their powers. Thus, according to Numbers 18:25–28, the priests, i.e., the sanctuary or the church, received one-tenth of the tithe. Their portion included also their share of some of the sacrifices, but the rest of the tithe went to the Levites, who were, among other things, the instructors of Israel (Deut. 33:10). The ecclesiastical realm was thus barred from becoming a power center. The same was true of the *civil* government, or the state. It was strictly limited in its powers because its tax was simply half a shekel a year for all males twenty years of age and over. We know from history that the covering (atonement, or protection) tax of Exodus 30:11–16 was the civil tax of Israel, of Judea, and of Jews at least into the Middle Ages.

Church and state were thus severely limited in their scope and power. The law of God is mainly addressed to covenant families, to the people of Israel. God's Kingdom order has this characteristic:

> After those days, saith the LORD, I will put my law in their inward parts, and write it in their hearts; and will be their God, and they shall be my people. (Jer. 31:33)

This means that the central area of action is within the covenant family and its members. The family is the cradle of life, man's first church, school, government, and vocation. God's law does not allow us to shift our duties onto the state or to the church. All such evasion of duty is lawlessness, according to Scripture, beginning with the care of one's parents. Our Lord declares:

> 6. … Well hath Esaias prophesied of you hypocrites, as it is written, This people honoureth me with their lips, but their heart is far from me.
> 7. Howbeit in vain do they worship me, teaching for doctrines the commandments of men.
> 8. For laying aside the commandment of God, ye hold the tradition of men, as the washing of pots and cups: and many other such like things ye do.
> 9. And he saith unto them, Full well ye reject the commandment of God, that ye may keep your own tradition.
> 10. For Moses said, Honour thy father and thy mother; and, Whoso curseth father or mother, let him die the death:
> 11. But ye say, If a man shall say to his father or mother, It is Corban, that is to say, a gift, by whatsoever thou mightest be profited by me; he shall be free.
> 12. And ye suffer him no more to do ought for his father or his mother;
> 13. Making the word of God of none effect through your tradition, which ye have delivered: and many such like things do ye. (Mark 7:6–13)

We must remember that, in speaking of *tradition*, our Lord refers to *man-made laws.*

The anthropologist Marvin Harris, in *Why Nothing Works, The Anthropology of Daily Life* (1987), witnesses against his own liberal views as he tells us of the growing breakdown of the modern world. The heart of the problem, he says, is our anti-natalism: we are anti-birth, and hence anti-life. Even those who are against abortion are sometimes marked by a meagerness of life and faith. Children are seen by too many people as a burden, not a blessing, a heritage from the Lord, and his reward (Ps. 127:3). Because of this anti-natalism and our inner meagerness, all the anti-life people, such as homosexuals and abortionists, have come out of the closet, and too many Christians have gone in.

This meagerness of soul has led to a church in retreat, a rapture or escape orientation, and to a general surrender of the world to the devil and his forces.

God's law is a plan and prescription for dominion in all of life. It is a statement of the means to victory by Christ's covenant people in their daily lives, in education, the family, the school, the arts and sciences, our vocations, in church, state, and everywhere else, including our health, for we are told that if we hearken to God's law,

> ...the LORD will take away from thee all sickness, and will put none of the evil diseases of Egypt, which thou knowest, upon thee; but will lay them upon all them that hate thee. (Deut. 7:15)

The law of God thus is a charter and constitution for a decentralized society in which the basic powers of government are exercised by God's covenant people in their self-government in every sphere, in their families, their vocations, the tithe agencies they create to minister to a variety of social problems and needs, and so on.

It cannot be stressed too heavily that social financing is a necessity. If God's covenant people do not provide it, then the state must and will. The present welfare state is in part due to the dereliction of Christians who have withdrawn the faith into the inner life of man. In those cultures where the state does not fund social services, brigandage takes over rapidly as the needy seize what they need: eighteenth-century England, for example, is evidence of this, and the death penalty for as many as two hundred plus offenses could not keep the hungry from stealing.

Wherever the Christian community abandons its necessary task of government and help, other forces take it over. Our Lord teaches us something we often do not choose to remember, that *service is power.*

> 25. … Ye know that the princes of the Gentiles exercise dominion over them, and they that are great exercise authority upon them.
> 26. But it shall not be so among you: but whosoever will be great among you, let him be your minister;
> 27. And whosoever will be chief among you, let him be your servant:
> 28. Even as the Son of man came not to be ministered unto, but to minister, and to give his life a ransom for many. (Matt. 20:25–28)

The word in verse 26 translated as "minister" is *diakonos,* servant, and in verse 27, "servant" translates *doulos,* slave, servant. Our Lord is emphatic: service is power, and the Gentiles fail to recognize this and so substitute the exercise of brute force for service. Today, however, the ungodly have borrowed from the church things the church often forgets, namely, that service is power. Hence, the modern state has created an unprecedented form of power by taking over the church's diaconal services. Rome provided bread and circuses to keep the mob from revolting. The modern state sees its social services as a means of creating a new paradise on earth, the Great Community or Society. The fallacy of its plan is that it cannot with all its money make a new creation out of sinful man: the state only aggravates and enhances man's sin by teaching him that it is the environment, not man, which is fallen and sinful.

The Christian must recognize that: *first,* man must be born again, and that there is no other way than Jesus Christ into God's Kingdom (John 3:3). *Second,* the living *act.* William Booth accused the churches of mummifying their converts, of producing mummy Christians who sat in the pew and whose action was little more than a meager reaching for one's wallet. When the Bible summons us to *hear* the word of the Lord, the word *hear* has the force of both hearing and obeying, of acting on God's orders.

Every word of Scripture is God's law. Because our Lord is God, and there is none other, every word of Scripture is a binding word, a command word, that requires us to hear and obey. We dare not reduce the faith to pious gush, nor worship to an aesthetic experience. The purpose of the church's services is not an impressive musical or liturgical treat but to provide marching orders to the soldiers of Christ.

> To the law and to the testimony: if they speak not according to this word, it is because there is no light in them. (Isa. 8:20)

T W O

The Unseen Enemy: Secular Humanism

Humanism is the second oldest religion known to man. It goes back to the Garden of Eden and to the tempter's creed as set forth in Genesis 3:1–5. Its *first* article of faith is the belief that all things, including every word from God, must be put to the test of man's reason and experience: "Yea, hath God said, ye shall not eat of every tree of the garden?" To take any word from God on faith is held to be irrationalism and bad religion. In the United States in 1987, a book by Osborn Segerberg, Jr., a Unitarian, takes a more favorable attitude towards Jesus than is common among American Unitarians. In *The Riddles of Jesus and the Answers of Science*, the author finds, he believes, "Modern Verification of His Wisdom and How It Can Help You" (subtitle to book). Segerberg takes a critical view of such Biblical scholar-critics as Reimarus, Strauss, Bauer, Weiss, and Schweitzer. Science, he holds, has confirmed many of the insights of Jesus, "a genius," and "In the Resurrection was the promise of the fate of all human beings." Segerberg does *not* see Jesus as the Son of God, as our atonement, nor as Lord, but rather as an evidence of human potentiality: Segerberg is a humanist. A humanist *can* at times believe in God to a degree, but basically as a resource for man rather than as Lord or Sovereign. Many churchmen who profess to believe the Bible from cover to cover are humanists who come to Christianity, not to be used by the Lord but to use Him. At the time of the American War of Independence, Samuel Hopkins saw the developing humanism of the church, with God as the great resource rather than Lord. He developed a test question for members and prospective members: "Are you willing to be damned for the glory of God?" He was not demanding hypocrisy, not anything more than to shock people into an awareness that we must seek *first* the Kingdom of God and His righteousness or justice (Matt. 6:33). We are saved to serve God and His glory, and this may mean the loss of many things. This means, in the words of Luther's hymn:

Let goods and kindred go,
This mortal life also;
The Body they may kill:
God's truth abideth still,
His kingdom is for ever.

The attitude, "Yea, hath God said?" tolerates only a positive word from God and man. It sees the chief end of God as serving man, so that man may enjoy himself forever. Humanism in the church sees Christ as our great fire and life insurance agent, *not as the Lord.*

The *second* article of faith for humanism is this, "Ye shall not surely die." It premises that it is possible that man's science, given enough time, will overcome the problems of death, together with all other social problems. This view separates death from sin, whereas Scripture is emphatic on their connection: by man's sin came death, and only by Christ's death and resurrection can atonement and resurrection come to man (1 Cor. 15:21, etc.). For the Christian, the connection of sin and death is inescapable, both for men and nations. Moreover, for us death is *not* a natural fact. God made all things very good (Gen. 1:31), but man's sin separated him from God and therefore life. Sin is the source of death, and death is a supernatural fact of judgment by the Almighty. As long as we view death in isolation from sin, and as a natural fact, we are prone to humanism.

Third, for the tempter and for humanism, his religion, it follows that disobedience to God is the beginning of wisdom: "in the day ye eat thereof, then your eyes shall be opened." He says thereby that, as long as we in faith believe and obey every word that proceeds from the mouth of God (Matt. 4:4), our eyes are *not* open, and we are blind. For humanism, faith in the Lord is the beginning of ignorance, and disobedience opens our eyes and makes us wise. We are told

> And when the woman saw that the tree was good for food, and that it was pleasant to the eyes, and a tree to be desired to make one wise, she took of the fruit thereof, and did eat, and gave unto her husband with her; and he did eat. (Gen. 3:6)

The tempter's counsel was, Be wise, apostatize!

Fourth, this wisdom means playing god: "ye shall be as gods, knowing good and evil." *To know* has here the force of *to determine:* ye shall determine for yourself what constitutes good and evil; every man will be his own source of law and morality. Instead of allowing God to provide them with all their laws, men will become their own law-makers. It is noteworthy that during the Commonwealth era, the New England missionary, John Eliot, converted and organized the Indians into self-governing villages, all ruled by God's law. On the accession of Charles II to the throne in 1660, the crown ministers ruled that royal law, not God's law, had to govern. The communities were broken up, and all copies of Eliot's *The Christian Commonwealth* were ordered burned by the public hangman. Only two copies survived.

The premise of modern culture the world over is Genesis 3:5, every man as his own god and law-giver. The death sentence pronounced on Adam stands against all nations, because they call such evils as abortion, homosexuality, and euthanasia good, and good, evil.

Humanism is commonly called *secular* humanism. The word *secular* has many meanings; the one of concern to us is, a layman, or, of the laity. Secular humanism is only in rare cases an openly avowed and/or an officially recognized state religion. Most frequently, it is the faith practiced by all too many men in the church and out of it, in the halls and courts of state, and in everyday life. Underneath the surface of established Christianity, secular humanism is widespread and commonly prevails.

As a result, we are in a cultural revolution. It is a revolution from the new man, Jesus Christ, to the old man, Adam, from supernatural man to fallen man. This is the culture of the Enlightenment, of Romanticism and Revolution, of Rousseau, and of our time.

This is a common opinion in our culture, that fallen man, as he is, is good, and he needs self-expression and gratification. Our rebellion against Christ reveals itself in the common idealization of primitive peoples. The Melanesians were cannibals. Transvestites and homosexuals are common among them. Their women suckle their young pigs at their breasts. Looking at these people, one naturalist has said, "It is wrong to force people to change." We, he declares, cannot teach these people the way of happiness. They could be our teachers in "being at peace with ourselves and our environment," and "their homes are sanctuaries of humanity." [1]

In line with this is the trend of state officers in the United States to view the Bible as a "child abuse handbook" because it calls for the disciplining and chastisement of unruly children. This attitude is even more pronounced in Sweden. The child is innocent, unfallen, and sacrosanct, and the Bible therefore is regarded as evil and unfit as a guide for family life.

---

1. Philippe Diol, *The Forgotten People of the Pacific* (New York: Barron's Educational Series, 1976), 255.

Herman Hoeksema stated powerfully the difference between the faith of fallen man and the faith of the redeemed:

> [T]he natural man would never give the answer which the Heidelberg Catechism puts in the mouth of its pupil in reply to the fifth question: "I am prone by nature to hate God and my neighbor." He is even offended at this truth. He far prefers his own philosophy. Man may fail occasionally. He may blunder. There may even be some that habitually sin. But inherently he is good. And he loves to extol his own virtues, and sing the praises of his good deeds in public. Only, it must be understood that this lie concerning himself, this closing of his eyes to the righteous judgment of God, is not due to any lack of natural light. The lie is an ethical one, not an intellectual mistake in judgment. Just as the "fool saith in his heart" that there is no God, so he persuades himself of his own goodness. Man lives in the sphere of the lie, both with regard to God and with respect to himself.[2]

There is an aspect of humanism, and of all anti-Christianity, which we must never forget: it is suicidal. Our Lord is the way, the truth, and the life: to be outside of Him is to be separated from life to death. We are told by Wisdom:

> 35. For whoso findeth me findeth life, and shall obtain favour of the LORD.
> 36. But he that sinneth against me wrongeth his own soul: all they that hate me love death. (Prov. 8:35–36)

The culture of humanism is thus a doomed one. The Lord declares, "Come out of her, my people, that ye be not partakers of her sins, and that ye receive not of her plagues" (Rev. 18:4). Humanism all around us is consuming the Christian capital of the Western world and is descending rapidly into disaster and death. Our humanistic culture resembles the tiny Pacific island republic of Nauru, with 3,600 millionaires. Nauru annually exports two million tons of phosphate, which means that

---

2. Herman Hoeksema, *The Triple Knowledge, An Exposition of the Heidelberg Catechism,* Vol. 1, (Grand Rapids, MI: Reformed Free Publishing Association, [1970] 1976), 67.

the island is rapidly disappearing. As of approximately 1976, three-fourths of the land had disappeared, and it has been estimated that by 1990, only bare rock will be left, no soil. The rich people of Nauru meanwhile have the highest consumption of alcohol in the Pacific, and their fifteen miles of highway have thousands of expensive automobiles.[3]

The Christian capital of the West is rapidly disappearing. Unless it is replenished, the West has no future and has nothing to give to the nations other than death. Rome fell because it was dead within. Seneca, a "moral" philosopher, led others into immorality. He was Nero's teacher in vice as well as philosophy. In the four peak years of his connections with power, he amassed a fortune of over $15,000,000, in terms of the value of the dollar of over a century ago. The sum of Seneca's wisdom was simply this: "The aim of all Philosophy is to despise life."[4] In our age too, various philosophies manifest a like temper. On the level of practice, we see anti-life as a reigning motive: abortion, homosexuality, euthanasia, and more. Fertility is seen as a problem by people who hate life. Another manifestation is the hatred of justice and of innocence. Lord Diplock of the British House of Lords a few years ago referred to the American rules of criminal law, and the suppression of evidence because of those rules, as a view of "the irrelevance of guilt." A California justice, Macklin Fleming, devoted a chapter in his study of *The Price of Perfect Justice* to "The Irrelevance of Guilt." [5] This should not surprise us: In a world at war with our Lord—a world that says, "Yea, hath God said?"—guilt has a privileged status among men who are themselves guilty before God. In one country after another, people are forbidden to speak the facts about criminal groups or classes, because they are more protected by law than are the law-abiding. I have heard it declared by professors and students that the Christian and white peoples of the world

---

3. Diol, *op. cit.*, 245.

4. Gerhard Uhlhorn, *The Conflict of Christianity with Heathenism*, from the third German edition (New York: Charles Scribner's Sons, 1879), 92f.

5. Macklin Fleming, *The Price of Perfect Justice* (New York: Basic Books, 1974), 121-128.

are the greatest force for evil known to history. The guilty are indicting the innocent, and the anti-Christians are insisting that Christ and the Bible are the root of all evil. In the United States, a daughter of one of America's more prominent families started a call girl service, a prostitution operation for the affluent male, using college girls. She justified herself, declaring that she was rendering a social service, and defining morality as hypocrisy.[6] Such attitudes are more and more commonplace, and even more, aggressively asserted. It has been rightly observed that, as the homosexuals came out of the closet, the Christians went in.

The Lord requires us to be *dominion men.* The Great Commission is a mandate to disciple all nations, teaching them the whole word of God (Matt. 28:18–20). It is called the Great Commission because it is a summation of the commission to Joshua, now expanded in scope from Palestine to the whole world. That commission declares in part:

> 3. Every place that the sole of your foot shall tread upon, that I have given unto you, as I said unto Moses.
> 5. There shall not any man be able to stand before thee all the days of thy life: as I was with Moses, so I will be with thee: I will not fail thee, nor forsake thee.
> 6. Be strong and of a good courage: for unto this people shalt thou divide for an inheritance the land, which I sware unto their fathers to give them.
> 7. Only be thou strong and very courageous, that thou mayest observe to do according to all the law, which Moses my servant commanded thee: turn not from it to the right hand or to the left, that thou mayest prosper whithersoever thou goest.
> 8. This book of the law shall not depart out of thy mouth; but thou shalt meditate therein day and night, that thou mayest observe to do according to all that is written therein: for then thou shalt make thy way prosperous, and then thou shalt have good success.

---

6. Sydney Biddle Barrows, with William Novak, *Mayflower Madam* (New York: Ballantine, Ivy Books, 1986), 51-52, 60-61, 170-71, 220, 314, 366.

9. Have not I commanded thee? Be strong and of a good courage; be not afraid, neither be thou dismayed: for the LORD thy God is with thee whithersoever thou goest. (Joshua 1:3, 5–9)

THREE

The Battle for a Generation: Focus on Education

In an interview shortly before his death, film director John Huston expressed his pessimistic view of life. Many of his films expressed this perspective, and Michael J. Bandler describes Huston's heroes as "losers every one." Huston himself said, "We're all losers. Not that I countenance death as a total loss, but we're all going to die."[1] In the United States, state schools include in their curriculum a "values clarification" emphasis which makes values and morality a subjective concern, not an objective standard, and they also include "death education." One consequence is a high suicide rate.[2]

None of this should surprise us. In any culture, two things most clearly reveal the religion of that society, *education and law.* Every legal system is an establishment of religion, and education transmits the faith and skills of a culture to its children. The religious institutions, i.e, church, synagogue, temple, or shrine, often represent a past faith. Because of the

1. Michael J. Bandler, "John Huston," in *American Way,* October 15, 1987, 134.

2. Samuel L. Blumenfeld, "The Lethal Education," in *The Blumenfeld Letter,* Vo. 2, No. 2, February, 1987.

institutional conservatism of religious organizations, the rites and forms remain when the faith is gone. Baptism, confirmation, and communion continue as before when the church is in reality humanistic. On the other hand, break-away churches often stress a limited aspect of the old faith: the forms of church government, a particular emphasis on doctrine, or a stress on religious experience. Wholeness is lost, and the new church is content to be a minor note in the culture rather than its shaper by the word and Spirit of God.

In the United States, the disaster to the wholeness of Biblical faith came with the rise in the early 1800s of "heart religion," with its emphasis on experience rather than a commanding world and life faith. According to James Turner, "heart religion" had four specific elements and/or consequences, all with roots in the seventeenth century realm of English thought. *First,* was "the assumption that knowledge became reliable only when verified in experience."[3] Such a view meant that revelation had to be tested by experience. It also made experience the standard in many realms where a very great measure of learning and understanding are necessary. Thus, it undermined authority as well as traditional wisdom. The ancient use of proverbs, the crystallization of the wisdom of centuries, began to wane sharply. The Bible as revelation began to give way to the Bible as a handbook for experiential religion. The faith was thus privatized, and creeds were shelved.

Then, *second,* in Turner's telling words,

> This rejection of traditional authority in favor of truths validated in experience bore on a second trait: the sense that empirical truths were more reliable than those that transcended physical reality.[4]

Experience and the here and now took priority over the authority of revelation. A sound and thorough knowledge of and belief in Scripture was condemned as "head religion," and

---

3. James Turner, *Without God, Without Creed, The Origins of Unbelief in America* (Baltimore, MD: The Johns Hopkins Press, 1985), 133.

4. Ibid., 134.

"heart religion" was held to be alone acceptable. Such a perspective gives more authority to present feelings than to ages-old revelation. It became routine to tell people that "head knowledge" and "head faith" were worthless and that what was *necessary* for salvation is a particular and dramatic form of "heart experience." Because of this view, Christian schools in the United States were downgraded and often opposed.

Third, a major consequence of such thinking was to *separate* precise, logical, and exact thinking from religion and to relegate it to a secular sphere.[5] Religion thus became the realm of feeling and pious gush, whereas science became the sphere of intelligence and knowledge. Instead of theology being the queen of the sciences, it was no longer even a science. Instead of commanding the world and life perspective in every sphere, Christianity became a minor part of the social order, and, instead of shaping the culture, was increasingly shaped by it. Instead of being a catholic or universal faith, Christianity became a minor and provincial one.

Fourth, it was as a result held that "knowledge evolved historically."[6] Anselm held, "I believe, in order that I may understand." This equation was now broken and replaced by two others. In the church, it was "I experience, in order that I may believe," and in the sciences, "I test, in order that I may understand." Both approaches are experiential; both reject the primary authority of revelation. Both hold that all things must be brought to man's heart or mind for an experiential test and approval.

At the same time, within the province of the state, certain parallel developments were under way. *First,* the state began to view education in messianic terms. The salvation of society was seen in terms of education, not regeneration. Instead of seeing salvation in terms of the new Adam, Jesus Christ, the statist educators saw it in terms of the learning given to the "natural" man, the old Adam and his humanity. The key to salvation was thus education, not regeneration. By imparting skills and learning to an unregenerate people, the state

5. Idem.
6. Ibid., 135.

increased the power and potentiality of their sin instead of checking it. A depraved man with a machine gun is far more deadly than one with a bow and arrow. The norm in education has been the acquisition of data per se, not a person with faith having both learning and wisdom.

Second, by this means, the *wholeness* of man was lost. Instead of a redeemed man fully equipped with learning and wisdom, education now worked to produce a man equipped with specialized learning and data but whose character was of little concern to the educators. As a result, we have educated learned monsters. Basic to godly education is an awareness of man as created in the image of God. The Westminster Shorter Catechism declares:

> A. 10. God created man male and female, after his own image, in knowledge, righteousness, and holiness, with dominion over the creatures. (Gen. 1:27–28; Col. 3:10, Eph. 4:24)

If we fail to educate in terms of the whole man, we warp men and society. Modern, humanistic education clearly disregards holiness. Its doctrine of righteousness or justice is humanistic and anti-Christian, as is its concept of knowledge. As for dominion, the goal is not the kingdom of God but of man, and it is thus also evil.

Third, the pattern for all men in Scripture is the new man, Jesus Christ. St. Paul tells us

> 29. For whom he did foreknow, he also did predestinate to be conformed to the image of his Son, that he might be the firstborn among many brethren.
> 30. Moreover whom he did predestinate, them he also called: and whom he called, them he also justified: and whom he justified, them he also glorified. (Rom. 8:29–30).

The goal is to be *conformed* to Jesus Christ, and this is God's decreed will for us. The humanists ridicule this conformity in favor of their own, an egalitarian doctrine which reduces man to the lowest common denominator instead of raising him to the level of the Lord of Glory, Jesus Christ. In 1960, L. P. Hartley's *Facial Justice* depicted a world in which the religion of equality had reached its logical conclusion. All men had to have standardized clothing and standardized plastic faces. Depersonalization was the law.[7] We see steps towards this goal already in laws which penalize any *factual* account of differences between religious and racial groups. In humanistic society the social demand downgrades man to the image of fallen men, in equality with all, instead of discipling him in terms of Christ.

Fourth, because humanistic education sees the "natural" or fallen man as the standard, it cannot tolerate a command moral law above and over man. It may tolerate Bible reading and more in the school, but its essential teaching is that all men must choose or create their own values and moral standards. Morality is seen as a subjective, not an objective, norm. Our values must serve us, not we the Lord. As a result, the sins of men become their values and their standards.

This means, *fifth,* that *sin becomes a right,* and humanistic education upholds man's "right" to do as he pleases as long as no physical violence is done to any man, although this limitation is now disappearing. The enthronement of sin as a right is very much with us today in such forms as abortion, homosexuality, and euthanasia, and its roots are all in Romanticism with its stress on the primacy of feeling, and the age of Revolution, with its belief that everything connected with the old order must be destroyed, and Christianity is seen as the epitome of the old order. An instance of the modern view of rights in the United States appeared in 1827, in Boston. According to William E. Nelson,

> The contagion of liberty even led to claims of license for immorality, when one frequenter of "the Hill" in Boston "pretended he had a right to visit all Whore-houses..."[8]

In education today, we face two hostile worldviews, Christianity versus humanism. The humanists are clearly wiser than

---

7. Chad Walsh, *From Utopia to Nightmare* (Westport, CT: Greenwood Press, [1962] 1976), 136.

8. William E. Nelson, *Americanization of the Common Law, The Impact of Legal Change on Massachusetts Society, 1760-1830* (Cambridge, MA: Harvard University Press, [1975] 1976), 90. Nelson's source is *Commonwealth v. Sosa, Boston Police Ct.*, 1827, n. 382.

the children of light: they know that the command of the future requires control over children and education.

The Biblical faith is clearly and plainly set forth for us in Psalm 127:3–5:

> 3. Lo, children are an heritage of the LORD: and the fruit of the womb is his reward.
> 4. As arrows are in the hand of a mighty man; so are children of the youth.
> 5. Happy is the man that hath his quiver full of them: they shall not be ashamed, but they shall speak with (or, *shall subdue,* as Ps. 18:47, or, *destroy*) the enemies in the gate.

The word translated as "speak with" is in Psalm 18:47 rendered *subdue* or *destroy*: "It is God that avengeth me, and subdueth the people under me." Children are a trust from God. We must all say with Hannah, the mother of Samuel,

> 27. For this child I prayed; and the LORD hath given me my petition which I asked of him:
> 28. Therefore also I have lent (or, *returned*) him to the LORD; as long as he liveth he shall be lent (or, *returned*) to the LORD. (1 Samuel 1:27–28)

Children are a God-given inheritance for our conquest of the world for Christ. They are a means of subduing the earth and exercising dominion under the Lord. If we give our children to state or private schools which are not systematically Christian in all their curriculum, we are then giving the future to God's enemies, and He will hold us accountable for laying waste our heritage. We thus must have Christian schools and Christian homeschools for the Lord's children. *We* are commanded to "bring them up in the nurture and the admonition of the LORD" (Eph. 6:4). This is a necessary step for that great consummation of God's will, announced beforehand for us in Revelation 11:15:

> The kingdoms of this world are become the kingdoms of our LORD, and of his Christ; and he shall reign for ever and ever.

FOUR

The Battle for Righteousness: The Application of Biblical Law to Secular Society

The battle for righteousness, or justice, must concern all Christians. Moreover, the only standard, source, or law of justice can be the law-word of God. We face a *secular* society. It is secular in the sense that it is not governed by priests or clergy, but by laymen, and it is also secular in that it is outside God's Kingdom and seeks a kingdom apart from the Lord.

In considering the *application* of God's law to such a society, we face two problems. *First,* the world is in revolt against our God and His law. Psalm 2:1–3 describes this world conspiracy against God:

> 1. Why do the heathen rage (or, tumultuously assemble, or conspire), and the people imagine a vain thing?
> 2. The kings of the earth set themselves, and the rulers take counsel together, against the LORD, and against his anointed, saying,
> 3. Let us break their bands asunder, and cast away their cords from us.

Second, the church is in revolt against God's law and sets it aside to a large degree. Too often churchmen are ready to listen to ugly misrepresentations of God's law, and to accept them. The law of God is seen as harsh, oppressive, and conducive to tyranny.

The fact is, however, that the total number of laws in Scripture are only a few hundred. All the rest of Scripture is to a degree a commentary on those laws, and the whole of the Bible makes up one none-too-large volume. The laws of the nations, and even of cities, fill libraries and are increased annually and often daily. Thus God's laws are few, and they provide for a *godly* free society. But this is not all. Many of God's laws are without any provision for penalties by man, the state, or the church. An example of this is *tithing*. In Malachi 3:8–12, we are told that God imposes penalties for failure to tithe, and blessings for faithfulness, but, here as elsewhere, men cannot play god and impose penalties.

The *purpose* of God's law is to provide government under God, not under men, not the church, nor the state. God's law is the means to a free and godly community. In surveying Biblical law, we must *first* recognize its premise. Fallen man can only create a sinful society and a tyrannical one. The goal of unregenerate man is a new Tower of Babel, Babylon the Great. It means playing God and controlling all things. The goal of regenerate man in Christ is the kingdom of God and the New Jerusalem, a realm wherein righteousness or justice dwells (2 Peter 3:13). Fallen man cannot build a just social order because he is in revolt against the God of *all* justice or righteousness and His law, which is justice. God's law is "the perfect law of liberty" (James 1:25), and it is a law hated by all who are in sin, which is slavery (John 8:31–36).

Second, for God's government and law to function, we must tithe. The tithe is God's tax, for His government. This tithe is then tithed to worship (Num. 18:25–28), so that the sanctuary receives one percent of a man's increase. Because civil government receives only half a shekel a year from all males twenty and over, it too, like the church, is limited. The rest of the tithe, as well as the poor tithe, goes for a variety of governmental functions, including education, health, and welfare.

The early church provided courts (in terms of 1 Corinthians 6:1ff.), inns for Christian travelers, homes for the needy and aged, hospitals, homes and schools for homeless children, ransom for captives, and more. Throughout Scripture, the test of faith includes ministering to people in distress. Our Lord declares, "Inasmuch as ye did it not to one of the least of these, ye did it not to me" (Matt. 25:45).

Third, the basic institution in Scripture is neither church nor state but rather the family. Because the family is God's basic institution, it is most protected by God's law. The offense of Biblical law in the eyes of many is its strict legislation to protect the family, because treason in Scripture, on the human scene, is to the family, *not* to the state. The modern concept of treason does not exist in the Bible. Because the family is the basic order of life, God's law guards the life of the family. The family is man's first and basic government, church, school, and vocation. Anthropologists and sociologists have recognized the centrality of the family in history. C. C. Zimmerman, in *Family and Civilization* (1947), classified families as trustee, domestic, or atomistic. The trustee family is basic to social order; the domestic family is still strong, but the state is given preeminence; the atomistic family marks the death of a society. The law of God requires a trustee family. The law is addressed to the covenant family, as in Deuteronomy, or in Proverbs. It requires the covenant people of God to establish God's order, beginning in their families.

Fourth, because God's order must be just or righteous, His people must have courts of justice. Hence, in 1 Corinthians 6:1ff., Christians are commanded to establish such courts. This they did, and soon provided justice in terms of God's law for believers and non-believers for many centuries. In the United States, Laurence Eck has reestablished Christian courts, and the results have been excellent.[1] The definition of *justice* in a humanistic court will not agree with God's law and

1. See Lynn R. Buzzard and Laurence Eck, *Tell it to the Church* (Wheaton, IL: Tyndale House Publishers, 1985).

justice. Hence, in a humanistic society, a separate court system becomes a necessity, and the Bible becomes the law book of such courts.

Fifth, according to Scripture, the penalty for crime is essentially restitution. In minor offenses, corporal punishment of a very limited sort is cited; in capital offenses, the death penalty is required. According to Exodus 22:1–17, restitution can be double or up to fivefold, depending upon the nature of the offense. *Forgiveness* in Scripture means, charges dropped because satisfaction has been rendered, or, charges deferred for the time being (Luke 23:34). Restitution thus means that there must be a restoration of God's order. If men do not enforce God's law as a nation, God will enforce it against them.

Sixth, a basic aspect of God's law is its concern for the earth. The land too must have its Sabbaths; war cannot be used as an excuse to destroy fruit trees and vines; sanitation is required, and more. Paul tells us about the goal for creation in God's plan of redemption:

> 19. For the earnest expectation of the creature waiteth for the manifestation of the sons of God.
> 20. For the creature was made subject to vanity, not willingly, but by reason of him who hath subjected the same in hope,
> 21. Because the creature itself also shall be delivered from the bondage of corruption into the glorious liberty of the children of God.
> 22. For we know that the whole creation groaneth and travaileth in pain together until now.
> 23. And not only they, but ourselves also, which have the firstfruits of the Spirit, even we ourselves groan within ourselves, waiting for the adoption, to wit, the redemption of our body. (Romans 8:19–23)

In our era, because of Pietism and its retreat into the inner man, we have lost this perspective. Let us remember that Calvin, while decrying idle speculation, insisted that Paul's words meant the resurrection of animals in God's glorious new creation. Let us remember too that God imposed seventy years of captivity on Judea for the seventy Sabbath years which had not been observed. Such laws were *not* a curiosity to our Christian forebears, and we dare not regard them as such now or ever.

Seventh, there is a very important thrust to God's law which we now disregard or spiritualize into meaninglessness. Paul echoes these laws in declaring, "I have learned, in whatsoever state I am, therewith to be content" (Phil. 4:11). Scripture says,

> 8. Remove far from me vanity [or, futility] and lies: give me neither poverty nor riches; feed me with food convenient for me,
> 9. Lest I be full, and deny thee, and say, Who is the LORD? Or lest I be poor, and steal, and take the name of my God in vain. (Prov. 30:8–9)

> 6. But godliness with contentment is great gain.
> 7. For we brought nothing into this world, and it is certain we can carry nothing out.
> 8. And having food and raiment let us be therewith content. (1 Tim. 6:6–8)

If we limit these words to their spiritual implication, we lose their full scope. In Deuteronomy 15:1–6, we are forbidden to go into debt, in times of need, for more than six years. The seventh or Sabbath year must also be a rest from debt. The goal is to live debt-free, to "owe no man anything, but to love one another" (Rom. 13:8). God's purpose for our lives is to live well because we live in faithfulness to Him.

Eighth, according to 1 John 3:4, "sin is the transgression of the law" (i.e., the law of God). The word translated as *sin* in this verse is defined as *anomia,* anti-law or lawlessness. Since God's law is righteousness or justice, to be a sinner is to oppose by action God's justice. Jesus Christ is our Savior *from sin to righteousness or justice.* We have been saved, says Paul, in order

> That the righteousness of the law might be fulfilled in us, who walk not after the flesh, but after the Spirit. (Rom. 8:4)

The law must be fulfilled, i.e., put into force, in us and through us. It is an error to teach that Christ saves us from hell; He saves us from sin and guilt. Hell is simply the logical conclusion of sin, of rebellion against God and His law: it is total separation from God.

Ours is a *secular* age because it wants no part of God. Remember, the death of God school of "theology" in the early 1970s did not say God is dead, but rather, God is dead for us, and we refuse to acknowledge whether He exists or not. *This is secularism.* If we refuse to live by every word that proceeds from the mouth of God (Matt. 4:14), then we too become secularists in this same sense.

The goal of God's Kingdom is the total holiness of all things. According to Zechariah 14:20–21,

> 20. In that day shall there be upon the bells of the horses, HOLINESS UNTO THE LORD; and the pots in the LORD's house shall be like the bowls before the altar.
> 21. Yea, every pot in Jerusalem and in Judah shall be holiness unto the LORD of hosts: and all they that sacrifice shall come and take of them, and seethe therein: and in that day there shall be no more the Canaanite in the house of the LORD of hosts.

FIVE

Humanism as It Affects the Family

One of the problems with the Christian pastorate is its concentration on the institutional church. Our Lord's command to us is broader: "Seek ye first the Kingdom of God, and his righteousness," or, justice (Matt. 6:33). Heaven and earth are alike God's creation, as are all spheres of life and activity, and hence all things must be governed by the word of God.

Too often, in its eagerness to build up the institutional church, which certainly needs such efforts, we neglect the other areas of our necessary ministry. Among these neglected areas is *the family*.

The family is God's basic institution. It is man's first church, first government, first school, and more. In Scripture, *all* the basic powers in society *save one* are given to the family. The sole exception is the death penalty, which tells us why Cain was not executed: all of humanity then was his immediate family. Some of these basic powers are the following: *First*, the control of children, which means the control of the future of a society, is given to the family. The state is increasingly usurping this power. *Second,* the control of property, which in Scripture follows neither a plan of private ownership, nor state ownership, but family ownership as a trust from the Lord. *Third,* inheritance is a family power. The covenant family builds up God's Kingdom by means of reserving its assets to the godly seed. The result is the capitalization of covenant man and God's Kingdom. The modern state is increasingly controlling both property and inheritance through taxation and regulation. *Fourth,* the fact of education is a major area of family authority and power, and here again the state has usurped family power. *Fifth,* the major welfare institution in all of history has been, and still is in many countries, the family.

Humanism, however, sees the family as a primitive form of social organization, which must, like the class or tribe, give way to the scientific organization of society by the state. Humanism recognizes that the family is a *natural* fact, a consequence of biology, mating, and parenting, but ancient and irrational natural forms must give way to more sophisticated and scientific forms. As a result, the family is increasingly controlled and regulated in order to allow the more scientific organization of society to prevail.

Van der Leeuw said of marriage:

> Marriage is "covenant" and "community" simultaneously: it is what is given *and* what is chosen. Its character as being something given becomes increasingly apparent to the degree that it expands into the family: choice, on the other hand, dominates it so far as it is a union of love. The common element that is sought, and at the same time discovered, is undifferentiated: it concerns the whole life…
>
> …These [the given and the chosen, RJR] are both expressed in the Biblical idea that the man leaves his father and mother for the sake of his wife—that is choice, but that God joins husband and wife together—that is givenness.[1]

---

1. Gerardus Van der Leeuw, *Religion in Essence and Manifestation* (New York: Macmillian, 1938), 244.

As Christians, we must say that both the givenness of marriage, and its status as a covenant, are from God and by His ordination. In the marriage ceremony as it exists in churches in the United States, the service or ritual has in it vows setting forth three contracts. *First,* the man and wife enter into a contract governed by both church and state by a variety of laws. The two together contract with the authorities. *Second,* the man and the woman enter into a covenant or contract each with the other. *Third,* the two together enter into a covenant with God and make vows to God, and to one another before God.

In humanistic marriage, *the given* is totally supplanted by the element of free *choice.* Whether a romantic union, a pragmatic one, or a mercenary marriage linking assets together, the emphasis is on the satisfaction and *the fulfillment* of the man and woman, and the purpose of divorce then becomes ungodly: if the goal is personal satisfaction, dissatisfaction is grounds for divorce.

In covenantal marriage, the purpose of the union is life in Christ and under God's law. According to Genesis 2:23–24,

> 23. And Adam said, This is now bone of my bones, and flesh of my flesh: she shall be called Woman, because she was taken out of Man.
> 24. Therefore shall a man leave his father and his mother, and shall cleave unto his wife: and they shall be one flesh.

These verses are to be understood in terms of the key fact about humanity and its being: creation in the image of God. According to Paul, in 1 Corinthians 11:8–12:

> 8. For the man is not of the woman; but the woman of the man.
> 9. Neither was the man created for the woman; but the woman for the man.
> 10. For this cause ought the woman to have power on her head because of the angels.
> 11. Nevertheless neither is the man without the woman, neither the woman without the man, in the Lord.

> 12. For as the woman is of the man, even so is the man also by the woman; but all things of God.

What we are told in these texts is, *first* of all, the God-centered character of marriage and the family: all things are from God and for His purposes. *Second,* Eve is created as Adam's helpmeet, not for Adam's sake per se, but in terms of man's calling to exercise dominion and to subdue the earth (Gen. 1:26–28). They are to be one life in terms of God's service. *Third,* because of this God-centered nature of marriage and the family, the woman has "power on her head." Like the angels, she has authority because she is under authority. In the old American West, women commonly wore bonnets even when working around the cabin because it was a statement to all strangers that they were under the protection of a man and deserved the protection of all godly men. Being hatless marked a prostitute from the days of Rome to the old West. *Fourth,* both the man and the woman are to be together and interdependent in the Lord. *Fifth,* children are one aspect of our inheritance in the Lord (Ps. 127:3–5).

Humanism sees marriage as, *first,* man-centered or state-centered, depending on the situation. From the days of Greece and Rome to the present, abortion has been seen as a solution to financial problems of over-population, and also at times strictly forbidden because the state needs soldiers and taxpayers. *Second,* because the purpose of marriage is reduced to self-fulfillment, marriage founders as both man and woman seek their own gratification. The children then are reared in terms of a like egocentricity. *Third,* both man and wife seek power apart from God and over each other. The eighteenth century saw the rise of man's "rights" over women, and the depressed status of women. In the Nineteenth and Twentieth Centuries, feminism and women's liberation movements have asserted the same irresponsible claims for women. We now have the children's rights movement to complete the decay of the family. *Fourth,* radical individualism governs men, women, and children. *Fifth,* children are no longer seen by many people as a blessing from God but as extensions of personal goals and pride. As a result, the family under humanism is in a state of crisis.

What is greatly needed within the Christian community is a restoration of the covenantal aspect of marriage and the family. Marriage is a covenant of law under God between a man and a woman. It places both under a Christ-centered sphere of life and responsibility (Eph. 5:21–33). Marriage as a covenant means that *the purpose and government* of marriage and the family is in terms of our calling as God's image bearers. The Westminster Shorter Catechism tells us:

> 10. God created man male and female, after his own image, in knowledge, righteousness, and holiness, with dominion over the creatures. (Gen. 1:27–28; Col. 3:10; Eph. 4:24)

The family in Christ is to be the key instrument for the growth of knowledge in its members, the furtherance of righteousness or justice, the development of holiness, and the exercise of dominion under God. Marriage must be seen as *more* than a natural fact, because it must be under a supernatural Lord and law, and it must be governed by more than nature.

SIX

Power and Service

Few things are more dangerous and also self-defeating than the common quest for power. It is a sad fact that the church has often been guilty of this same lust for power and has warped its doctrines to justify its ways. To illustrate, churches have at times taken a legitimate area of faith and practice and used it to justify their power. Thus, more than a few communions have confined the workings of the Holy Spirit to the church's channels, i.e., to the clergy, to their form of the sacraments, and to the church's decisions. In other instances, churchmen have insisted on a close connection between their form of evangelistic revivalism and the working of the Holy Spirit. Thus. D. M. Lloyd-Jones observed, with respect to Charles G. Finney's influence and the fact of revivals,

> Finney's whole outlook and teaching seems to have become a governing factor in the outlook of the church. It has led to the notion of what we call "evangelistic campaigns." Finney is the man of all men who is responsible for the current confusion with regard to this matter. Our

> American brethren even get confused about the very terms. They talk about "holding a revival meeting"; they mean, of course, an evangelistic campaign. That is the result of Finney's influence, and it has really befogged the whole situation. The influence of Finney's teaching upon the outlook of the church has been quite extraordinary. People now, instead of thinking instinctively about turning to God and praying for revival when they see that the church is languishing, decide rather to call a committee, to organize an evangelistic campaign, and work out and plan an advertising programme to "launch" it, as they say. The whole outlook and mentality has entirely changed.[1]

In American revivalism, the Holy Spirit is too often tied to a particular form and strategy. In the early 1800s, it was common to identify a particular form of conversion experience with the Holy Spirit. Those not having that experience were regarded as unconverted, even though the clear evidence indicated they were men of strong faith.

The same humanistic approach is apparent with respect to *faith.* Paul gives us a very clear statement of the meaning of faith in Ephesians 2:8–10:

> 8. For by grace are ye saved through faith; and that not of yourselves: it is the gift of God.
> 9. Not of works, lest any man should boast.
> 10. For we are his workmanship, created in Christ Jesus unto good works, which God hath before ordained that we should walk in them.

Faith is not a human attribute. It is a divine and supernatural grace. It cannot be seen as a human power, nor exercised in contempt of God's law-word. God makes clear, in Deuteronomy 15:1–11, that long-term debt is wrong, and that, normally, we are to live debt-free: "Owe no man anything, but to love one another" (Rom. 13:8). In the United States, at least, it has now become routine to regard debt as an act of faith. I am regularly told that going into debt is evidence of faith and a trust

1. D. M. Lloyd-Jones, *The Puritans: Their Origins and Successors* (Edinburgh, Scotland: Banner of Truth Trust, 1987), 5.

in the Lord. Countless churches and ministries are radically in debt and make pleas of desperation to their supporters. They declare that the honor of God is at stake, and so on. The radio and television preachers, charismatic and non-charismatic, are similar in their financial operations: they live by debt. People close to these organizations have told me that, no matter how many millions of dollars pour in, debts are not retired but rather increased. The leaders see ever-increasing plunges into debt as evidence of greater faith. One man, close to these various leaders, told me once in dismay that debt has replaced the Holy Spirit in the lives of these men: they *need* increasing debt to energize them. They derive their drive and power from the pressures of debt rather than from the Holy Spirit.

In Psalm 62, David gives us the doctrine of power which we must consider:

> 1. Truly my soul waiteth upon God: from him cometh my salvation.
> 2. He only is my rock and my salvation; he is my defence; I shall not be greatly moved.
> 3. How long will ye imagine mischief against a man? ye shall be slain all of you: as a bowing wall shall ye be, and as a tottering fence.
> 4. They only consult to cast him down from his excellency: they delight in lies: they bless with their mouth, but they curse inwardly. Selah.
> 5. My soul, wait thou only upon God; for my expectation is from him.
> 6. He only is my rock and my salvation: he is my defence; I shall not be moved.
> 7. In God is my salvation and my glory: the rock of my strength, and my refuge, is in God.
> 8. Trust in him at all times; ye people, pour out your heart before him: God is a refuge for us. Selah.
> 9. Surely men of low degree are vanity, and men of high degree are a lie: to be laid in the balance, they are altogether lighter than vanity.
> 10. Trust not in oppression, and become not vain in robbery: if riches increase, set not your heart upon them.

> 11. God hath spoken once; twice have I heard this; that power belongeth unto God.
> 12. Also unto thee, O Lord, belongeth mercy: for thou renderest to every man according to his work.

David speaks here as a man in distress, facing the hostile powers of this world. In verses 1–4, he is calmly resigned to trust in God, although faced with cruel animosity. He has strength: God is his rock and salvation. According to Leupold, the Hebrew of verse 1a must be rendered, "Only unto God silence my soul."[2] In trust and without complaint, he places himself in God's hands, and this is his recognition of God's strength. In verses 5–8, David summons us to do the same. God is on His throne, and therefore we should not be shaken. In verses 9–12, all other help than the Lord's is futile, or vain, David says, and his confidence rests on this fact: that *power belongs to God.* The Lord gives us power, godly power, only as we believe and obey Him. We are not to trust in riches nor oppression, nor men, for men of high and low estates are alike untrustworthy and vain. God takes authority from men who abuse it to give it to others (Matt. 21:43; cf. 8:12).

Power and authority on the human scene are delegated from God to man for God's purposes. Our Lord defines for us the meaning of power and dominion:

> 25. But Jesus called them unto him, and said, Ye know that the princes of the Gentiles exercise dominion over them, and they that are great exercise authority upon them.
> 26. But it shall not be so among you: but whosoever will be great among you, let him be your minister;
> 27. And whosoever will be chief among you, let him be your servant:
> 28. Even as the Son of man came not to be ministered unto, but to minister, and to give his life a ransom for many. (Matt. 20:25–28)

---

2. H. C. Leupold, *Exposition of the Psalms* (Columbus, OH: Wartburg Press, 1959), 459.

The Lord tells us that *godly service is power.* Ours is a ministry, and our Lord sets the pattern thereof. Scripture tells us two things in this regard. *First,* in the foot-washing incident at the Lord's Last Supper, we read

> 13. Ye call me Master and Lord: and ye say well: for so I am.
> 14. If I then, your Lord and Master, have washed your feet; ye also ought to wash one another's feet.
> 15. For I have given you an example, that ye should do as I have done to you.
> 16. Verily, verily I say unto you, the servant is not greater than his lord; neither he that is sent greater than he that sent him.
> 17. If ye know these things, happy are ye if ye do them. (John 13:13–17)

Two common errors have been drawn from these words. On the one hand, many have believed that a ritual foot-washing must be observed by the church. In the past, bishops and kings have practiced this rite, and, in some churches today, it is a continuing ritual. We are better at maintaining forms than meaning. On the other hand, some have felt that the pastor is obligated to be the congregation's handyman. In another text, we see the problem as the early church resolved it:

> 1. And in those days, when the number of the disciples was multiplied, there arose a murmuring of the Grecians against the Hebrews, because their widows were neglected in the daily ministration.
> 2. Then the twelve called the multitude of the disciples unto them, and said, It is not reason that we should leave the word of God and serve tables.
> 3. Wherefore, brethren, look ye out among you seven men of honest report, full of the Holy Ghost and wisdom, whom we may appoint over this business.
> 4. But we will give ourselves continually to prayer, and to the ministry of the word. (Acts 6:1–4)

This text tells us, *first,* that, from its infancy, the Christian community was a community, a *family.* The needy were cared for and fed. While still a limited and poor group, these Christians cared for one another in all material needs. *Second,* while not intentional, the disciples, knowing better the needs of the Hebrew-speaking widows, tended for this reason to neglect the Greek-speaking widows. Being overworked, they erred. *Third,* they recognized that the centrality of their calling would be lost if they neglected prayer and the ministry of the word for charity. They did not thereby downgrade charity, but gave it more importance by establishing the diaconate to care for the needy. We know from Acts that the apostolic concern for the sick and the needy remained, but there was now a separate ministry to concentrate on it. Let us remember too that, in the early church, a deacon's calling was a full-time ministry also, because the ministry of service was so important.

The *power* of the early church was in its remarkable ministry of service to the needy, to widows and orphans, to the sick, the homeless, and to travelers. Captives were ransomed, discarded newly-born babies picked up and reared, and much, much more. It was the power of obedience. I called attention earlier to the equation by many television evangelists of going into debt with having faith. Such an equation is sinful and blasphemous. Faith does *not* mean going into debt in the trust that God will bail us out because we are His people and it is His work. Our Lord, in the temptation, gives us the model of faith: obedience.

> It is written, Man shall not live by bread alone, but by every word that proceedeth out of the mouth of God. (Matt 4:4)

> It is written again, Thou shalt not tempt the Lord thy God. (Matt. 4:7)

> It is written, Thou shalt worship the Lord thy God, and him only shalt thou serve. (Matt 4:10).

God does not honor a false faith. He does not honor vast edifices and enterprises built on ungodly debt. In Deuteronomy 28:1–68, we see in verses 2 and 15 that God's *irresistible blessings* will pursue and overtake us if we are faithful, even as His *irresistible curses* will pursue and overtake us if we are disobedient to His law-word.

We are thus summoned away from the humanistic quest for power to the recognition that godly power means faithfulness, obedience, to our Lord. It means the love of God, and the love of our neighbor, with all our heart, mind and being.

We dare not lose the connection between faith and obedience, because we then render our faith into no more than "a tinkling cymbal" (1 Cor. 13:1). We are plainly told:

> By their fruits ye shall know them. (Matt 7:20)

> Do we then make void the law through faith? God forbid: yea, we establish the law. (Rom. 3:31)

> For as the body without the spirit is dead, so faith without works is dead also. (James 2:26)

SEVEN

THE CHURCH OF THE WARM FUZZIES VS. THE CHURCH OF JESUS CHRIST

Recently, when my wife, Dorothy, and Mrs. Grayce Flanagan were having tea they began a discussion of Christianity and the church. Their terminology was so telling that it was in and of itself a superb analysis of our problem. Churches and their members were classified as members of one or another of two groups: "the warm fuzzies," and the warriors. "The warm fuzzies" are all who reduce the faith to a warm and happy feeling and who want the faith to make them "feel good inside." Ministers and churches are rated in terms of their satisfaction of the need for a warm and fuzzy feeling. Precision in doctrine is seen as hostile to warmth, whereas fuzzy thought leaves room for a preoccupation with feeling. On the other hand, the warriors want to see the Kingdom of God and His justice govern men and nations. Their joy is in the truth of God. They want to *live and act* for Christ, but, if need be, they are ready to say, "Though he slay me, yet will I trust in him" (Job 13:15). The Church of the Warm Fuzzies is too much with us. As a result, the church is impotent; instead of shaping history, it is shaped by it. Instead of acting on the world scene, it reacts. Serous questions must be raised about such a church, because a powerless church seems to be a contradiction in terms. A persecuted church is attacked because it is a power center, and an enemy of Christ's enemies.

One of the finest statements of our problem comes from Pope Benedict XV (1914–1922), who in "Humani Generis Redemptionem," June 15, 1917, an encyclical on preaching the word of God said:

> 3. The causes of these evils are varied and manifold: no one, however, will gainsay the deplorable fact that the ministers of the Word do not apply thereto an adequate remedy. Has the Word of God then ceased to be what it was described by the Apostle, living and effectual and more piercing than any two-edged sword? Has long-continued use blunted the edge of that sword? If that weapon does not everywhere produce its effects, the blame certainly must be laid on those ministers of the Gospel who do not handle it as they should. For no one can maintain that the Apostles were living in better times than ours, that they found minds more readily disposed towards the Gospel or that they met with less opposition to the law of God.[1]

We need constantly to recommission ourselves by turning to Scripture, not for what we can get out of it for our use, but for what God declares about His use of us. A statement by Paul to the philosophers of Athens is very important in this context:

> 22. Then Paul stood in the midst of Mars' hill, and said, Ye men of Athens, I perceive that in all things ye are too superstitious.
> 23. For as I passed by, and beheld your devotions, I found an altar with this inscription, TO THE UNKNOWN GOD. Whom therefore ye ignorantly worship, him declare I unto you.
> 24. God that made the world and all things therein, seeing that he is Lord of heaven and earth, dwelleth not in temples

1. Claudia Carlen, IHM, *The Papal Encyclicals, 1903-1939* (A Consortium Book, McGrath Publishing Company, 1981), 154.

made with hands;
25. Neither is worshipped with men's hands, as though he needed any thing, seeing he giveth to all life, and breath, and all things;
26. And hath made of one blood all nations of men for to dwell on the face of the earth, and hath determined the times before appointed, and the bounds of their habitation;
27. That they should seek the Lord, if haply they might feel after him, and find him, though he be not far from every one of us:
28. For in him we live, and move, and have our being; as certain also of your own poets have said, For we are also his offspring.
29. Forasmuch then as we are the offspring of God, we ought not to think that the Godhead is like unto gold, or silver, or stone, graven by art and man's device.
30. And the times of this ignorance God winked at; but now commandeth all men every where to repent:
31. Because he hath appointed a day, in the which he will judge the world in righteousness by that man whom he hath ordained: whereof he hath given assurance unto all men, in that he hath raised him from the dead.
(Acts 17:22–31)

I have actually heard fundamentalist preachers say that Paul's sermon was a failure because he did not preach John 3:16! In reality, Paul's sermon on Mars' Hill was a total and direct challenge to all that Greco-Roman society and philosophy represented; it was a pronouncement which spelled the end of that world, and hence many of Paul's listeners could not bear to hear him any further. What did Paul say? Remember, their interest was aroused by Paul's talk about the resurrection of Jesus. As Cornelius Van Til, in *Paul at Athens,* has shown, the Greeks were interested in novel ideas such as the resurrection of the dead, but only if such freakish or unusual events were seen as evidence of the potentiality of being, or, in more modern terms, as evidence of the next step in evolution. As against this, Paul said, *first,* there is a Creator God who is more than the God of Plato and Aristotle, a mere limiting concept. He is the living God; however much you may choose not to know Him, He is the Creator, Lord, and Governor of all things. All men and nations are His creation, and answerable to Him. This means, *second*, that there is a day of judgment for all men when the resurrected Jesus shall judge men and nations. God summons all men to repent before that day, or face the justice of Christ's court. *Third*, all men must worship God, not in ignorance nor according to their appointed ways, but in terms of God's revealed word and requirement. Any other worship is will-worship. It is the philosopher's version of the warm fuzzies. *Fourth*, Paul uses sentences from Greek writers in this sermon to give them a radically different content. Whether the altar inscription, or a line from the poets, he emptied out the Greek content to give a Biblical one instead. The key line is this: "For in him we live, and move, and have our being." For the Greeks and Romans, the divine-human milieu was *the state*. It was the center, the stage of history and of "eternity," whatever that might be. The *polis* or city-state was not eternal, because, for the Greeks nothing truly was, but it was the arena of action for men and whatever gods might be. As Gillespie has pointed out,

> The polis is the place of human life, and those who live outside it, as Aristotle maintained, are for the Greeks either beasts or gods. Man is the *zoon politikon*, the political animal, and whatever immortality is granted him as a man must be bound up with the polis ... Thus it is not the eternality of the polis that is the source of human immorality. Human immortality is rather bound up with the polis because the polis is the place of speech, the place in which the eternal is brought to light in the actual through speech.[2]

Paul challenged this whole doctrine, and, in time, Pauline thought shattered it. Men began to know, as they came to a saving knowledge of Jesus Christ as Lord, that He is the Lord

---

2. Michael Allen Gillespie, *Hegel, Heidigger, and the Ground of History* (Chicago, IL: University of Chicago Press, 1984), 3.

of history, that we live and move and have our being in the triune God. From the earliest days of the church, the baptismal confession required of all believers came from Paul, and it was simply this: Jesus Christ is Lord. This was a denial that Caesar is lord, the confession required by Rome. It was a denial that we must live and move and have our being in the state, in Rome, Britain, or the United States, because all nations live under Christ, who has, *for all nations,* "determined the times before appointed, and the bounds of their habitation." If they will not seek Him, and obey Him, they shall be judged by Him. Paul declares also

> 9. Wherefore God also hath highly exalted him, and given him a name which is above every name:
> 10. That at the name of Jesus every knee should bow, of things in heaven, and things in earth, and things under the earth:
> 11. And that every tongue should confess that Jesus Christ is Lord, to the glory of God the Father. (Phil. 2:9–11)

The Greco-Roman world gave way before the word of Paul on Mars' Hill to become Christendom, wherein, for all their faults, men lived, moved, and had their being in the triune God.

The modern age has seen a reversal of Paul's work. This has been especially true since Hegel, who held, "The state is the divine idea, as it is present-at-hand on earth."[3] Man once again is a political animal, not a man created in God's image. Too often the critical question is, are you a conservative or a socialist? Not, are you saved or lost. We set forth, not the image of God's redeemed and faithful, but the image of a citizen of the United States, Britain, France, or some other state. We have a false standard of identification. We have remade ourselves in Aristotle's image as political animals. Now, in the state we live and move and have our being, and also our death. Instead of dying in Christ, we die in the state, or Medicare, or the National Health Plan, not in terms of godly care but statist

3. Hegel, *Philosophy of History,* 12:56-57, cited in Gillespie, 91.

care. We no longer provide the health, education, and welfare in society because the state is now our good shepherd. We have accepted the reversal of Paul's declaration of man's freedom from sin and men, and we are content to let the humanistic dream of social order govern us.

The question which confronts us is this: In whom do we live and move and have our being? Are we Christians, or Hegelian Greeks? The question we face on Judgment Day is the same: In whom did you live and move and have your being? In Christ, or in Caesar? If in Christ, then every area of life and thought must be brought under His dominion, and into obedience to His law-word.

The Church of the Warm Fuzzies is no place for the men of whom Paul speaks:

> 31. What shall we then say to these things? If God be for us, who can be against us?
> 32. He that spared not his own Son, but delivered him up for us all, how shall he not with him also freely give us all things?
> 33. Who shall lay anything to the charge of God's elect? It is God that justifieth.
> 34. Who is he that condemneth? It is Christ that died, yea rather, that is risen again, who is even at the right hand of God, who also maketh intercession for us.
> 35. Who shall separate us from the love of Christ? Shall tribulation, or distress, or persecution, or famine, or nakedness, or peril, or sword?
> 36. As it is written, For thy sake we are killed all the day long; we are accounted as sheep for the slaughter.
> 37. Nay, in all these things we are more than conquerors through him that loved us.
> 38. For I am persuaded, that neither death, nor life, nor angels, nor principalities, nor powers, nor things present, nor things to come,
> 39. Nor height, nor depth, nor any other creature, shall be able to separate us from the love of God, which is in Christ Jesus our Lord. (Rom. 8:31–39)

EIGHT

THE CHAMBERS OF POWER

An interesting comment in John Morgan's study of certain aspects of Puritan life and thought concerns their emphasis:

> Much of the puritan attempts at reform, perhaps especially in Elizabethan times, concentrated on the chambers of power. But even from the beginning of our period puritans were also keen to proselytize at the lowest organizational levels; hence a new interest arose in the possibility of the household as a center of godly instruction. At the bottom of all social analysis came the family rather than the individual.[1]

The enduring power of Puritanism came as it recognized that *the chambers of power* are not the same in reality as those seen by the world as the seats of dominion and authority. One of the major current problems is our failure to recognize the chambers of power which are readily available to all of us.

---

1. John Morgan, *Godly Learning, Puritan Attitudes towards Reason, Learning and Education, 1560-1640* (Cambridge, England: Cambridge University Press, 1986), 142.

The historian Ernst Breisach, in his excellent study of *Historiography, Ancient, Medieval, and Modern* (1983), notes with respect to the future as Jacob Burckhardt saw it,

> As ever new attempts would have to be made to achieve equality among people who by nature were unequal, traditions, laws, and values would be destroyed as roadblocks on the way to absolute equality until, finally, social stability would disappear. In order to restore that stability and achieve ultimate equality people would call upon socialism with its ever-increasing regimentation and centralization; this was a perfect situation for the emergence of despots—the terrible simplifiers—who offered order without true legitimacy and tradition. In such a new society tradition and with it history would be replaced as society's guides by fickle public opinion and quickly changing fashions of thought.[2]

We are in that "future" now. Men are working to replace Christianity with humanism in every sphere of life and thought. Whatever the cost, man's will must be done. The West, long governed by God's law, is now under man's law. As early as 1924 in the United States, one of the most eminent legal scholars, in surveying the work begun in the second half of the nineteenth century, declared:

> Thus the cycle is complete. We are back to the state as the unchallengeable authority behind legal precepts. The state takes the place of Jehovah handing the tables of the law to Moses...[3]

"The state takes the place of Jehovah": this is the proud boast of a major legal authority.

The Chronicles of Livonia, in the second quarter of the thirteenth century, tells us of the people's desire to rid themselves of Christianity. They sought to reverse their baptism by

---

2. Ernst Breisach, *Historiography, Ancient, Medieval, and Modern* (Chicago, IL: University of Chicago Press, 1983), 304.

3. Roscoe Pound, *Law and Morals* (Chapel Hill, NC: The University of North Carolina Press, 1924), 14.

bathing in the Dvina River, to remove their baptism by a water ritual and to send their baptism back into Germany.[4] In the twentieth century, men have sought by the mass murders of Christians to reverse history and reestablish pagan man. In fact, Eugen Rosenstock-Huessy, in *Out of Revolution, Autobiography of Western Man* (1938), sees Western history as for some centuries now a revolt against the supernatural man, Jesus Christ, and an effort to reestablish natural man, an Adam in Rousseau's image. We are thus in a war, a war against Christ, and the enemy proudly claims all the chambers of power. How are we to survive this assault, let alone regain freedom and power? But there are other questions as well. The enemy holds all the established chambers of power but is still failing. The world lurches from crisis to crisis, and men's hearts fail them for fear. Are these chambers now not in themselves chambers of impotence and petty tyranny rather than true authority and power? The bankruptcy of humanistic statism confronts us on all sides. One American state senator described to me a few years ago the growing fearfulness of many legislators, even as they triumph, because they see the failures of their measures. The powers that be, he said, have "battle diarrhea." Their hearts fail them for fear!

Our recourse in such a time as this must be to the true chambers of power, to the power of God's word and Spirit. It is our Lord Himself who declares, as He prays,

> 17. Sanctify them through thy truth: thy word is truth.
> 18. As thou hast sent me into the world, even so have I also sent them into the world.
> 19. And for their sakes I sanctify myself, that they also might be sanctified through the truth. (John 17:17–19)

Our Lord states that victory requires complete consecration. The word sanctify can be rendered also as consecrate, or hallow. Every power, ability, and means must be rendered to God and His Kingdom. As Westcott noted, "It is not enough for the

---

4. Breisach, *op.cit.*, 110.

Christian to be 'kept' (vv. 11, 15); he must also advance."[5] Moreover,

> The "truth" is not only a power within him by which he is moved; it is an atmosphere in which he lives. The end of the truth is not wisdom, which is partial, but holiness, which is universal.[6]

This universal holiness is the bringing of every area of life and thought into captivity to Christ as Lord, as King of all creation.

While truth carries with it grace, it does *not* mean compromise. The early church was not weakened but rather strengthened by doctrinal controversies: it knew that union is not necessarily unity, a fact that the ecumenical movement today disregards.

Dogmatism in our times has a bad meaning. The dictionary defines it as "1. Positive or arrogant assertion, as of belief, without proof. 2. *Philos.* An uncritical faith in the presumptions of reason or a priori principles." The root word, *dogma,* is, we are usually told, a Greek word meaning *opinion*; in reality, it commonly meant an authoritative decree or ordinance. It is in this sense that we are to understand Christian dogma and dogmatics, of which Gerald Bray has written:

> Properly understood in this way, Christian dogmatism is the greatest force for freedom which mankind has ever known. By claiming the mind for God, dogmatism shatters the bounds of the natural world which imprison the creative imagination and distort scientific analysis. It makes a relapse into sentimentality and vagueness in the name of religion impossible. It attacks the philosophies of the world and denies the claims of atheistic and amoral logic to rule the lives of men. Dogmatism abhors indifference and agnosticism, and demands considered commitment from those who would follow Christ.[7]

---

5. Brooke Foss Westcott, *The Gospel According to St. John* (Grand Rapids, MI: Eerdmans, [1885] 1954), 245.

6. Idem.

7. Gerald Bray, *Creeds, Councils, and Christ* (Leicester, England: Inter-Varsity Press, 1984), 37.

We are the people of light, and we are not permitted by our Lord to keep our light under a bushel basket (Matt. 5:15). The chambers of power for us are the places appointed to us by the Lord, to exercise dominion where we are in terms of the image of God in us, in knowledge, righteousness or justice, and with holiness (Gen. 1:27–28; Col. 3:10; Eph. 4:25).

We have too long imagined that the chambers of power are outside of Christ and in the possession of the world. Men's chambers of power are all towers of Babel, excellent guarantees of confusion and judgment rather than of true dominion. When men believe in man, they will look to man for answers, whereas when men believe in God, they will know that His Son and word provide us with the answers and the power.

As Rome advanced in its humanism, it also progressed, as had Greece, in its recourse to magic and other like answers. The solutions *had* to come from the natural world. Gerhard Uhlhorn described the lengths to which they went:

> Women and children were cut open alive in the palace of Diocletian's coregent, in order to inspect their entrails. Numerous amulets were worn to protect from magic. Omens and signs were diligently observed. Of almost every Emperor portents which predicted his reigning are narrated by his contemporaries. In the life of Diocletian one of the most important events was the prophecy of a Druidess, who foretold that he would be Emperor, when he was only a subaltern in the army near Lutetia (Paris). Maximinus Daza never made any change without an omen; he did not even go out without consulting his Chaldean book of hours. The interpretation of dreams was pursued with especial zeal. Artemidorus of Ephesus spent his whole life in investigating all that had been written on dreams, and even took long journeys to collect experiences and materials. The result was his book *Oneirocritica*, the interpretation of dreams. In it, dreams are divided, with a semblance of science, into definite classes, and then their meaning is given. If one has a dream of a great head, that signifies riches and honors to such as have them not, otherwise it portends

> care. Long and smooth hair signifies happiness, short hair misfortune; wool instead of hair, sickness; a short head, misery. If a man dreams that ants creep into his ear, that signifies many hearers to an orator, but death to other men, for ants come out of the earth.[8]

This was the science of the Roman world, and our contemporary scientific mythology, whether in psychiatry or biology, is often equally absurd.

The religion of Rome was the imperial cult.[9] The emperors were the lords of the chambers of power and hence were worshipped as gods. A statue of Caesar bore the inscription, "To the unconquered God."[10] Both rich and poor saw divinity in the statist chambers of power.

But it was men like Paul, beaten, in prison, and facing death often,

> 24. Of the Jews five times received I forty stripes save one.
> 25. Thrice was I beaten with rods, once was I stoned, thrice I suffered shipwreck, a night and a day I have been in the deep;
> 26. In journeying often, in perils of waters, in perils of robbers, in perils by mine own countrymen, in perils by the heathen, in perils in the city, in perils in the wilderness, in perils in the sea, in perils among false brethren;
> 27. In weariness and painfulness, in watchings often, in hunger and thirst, in fastings often, in cold and nakedness.
> 28. Beside those things that are without, that which cometh upon me daily, the care of all the churches.
> (2 Cor. 11:24–28)

It was men like Paul who held the true chambers of power, and who triumphed.

Our Lord is the same Lord as Paul's. We have now the complete revelation, the whole word of God. We have the self-

---

8. Gerhard Uhlhorn, *The Conflict of Christianity with Heathenism* (New York, NY: Charles Scribner's Sons, 1879; from the third German edition), 317-18.

9. Donald Earl, *The Age of Augustus* (New York, NY: Exeter Books, [1968] 1980), 166ff.

10. Ibid., 173.

same Spirit of God, the Spirit of power. We have a mandate to bring *all things* into captivity to Christ.

Where will we seek power, in the false chambers, or in Christ?

NINE

Hope and Victory

A generation ago, one prominent American was aptly described as a trumpet that always sounds retreat. There are too many such men among us. When they are, as this man was, men without faith, this should not surprise us. Paul tells the Ephesians that, before their conversion,

> ... at that time ye were without Christ, being aliens from the commonwealth of Israel, and strangers from the covenants of promise, having no hope, and without God in the world. (Eph. 2:12)

Arthur S. Way, in his translation, renders the verse in these words:

> Remember that you were in those days excluded from all part in the Messiah, counted aliens from the nationality of Israel, foreigners without share in the covenants given by God's promise. You had no hope, you were without God in that heathen world of yours.[1]

1. Arthur S. Way, trans., *The Letters of St. Paul* (London, England: Macmillan, [1901] 1935), 180-81.

Paul's statement is regularly misread to say that the unbeliever has no hope of God insofar as heaven is concerned. But what Paul says is that the ungodly have *no hope in this world.* Bishop Westcott commented on this verse,

> There is a strange pathos in the combination. They were of necessity face to face with all the problems of nature and life, but without Him in whose wisdom and righteousness and love they could find rest and hope. The vast, yet transitory, order of the physical universe was for them without its Interpreter, an unsolved enigma.
>
> The Gentiles had, indeed, "gods and lords many," but no GOD loving men and Whom men could love.[2]

Very bluntly, what Paul tells us is this: it is a mark of ungodliness, of being alien to God, to be without hope in this world. The equation is, without God, without hope, in *this* world as well as in the world to come. To have no hope is to be ungodly. Paul tells us in Romans 5:1–5 that, when we are the redeemed of God in Christ, tribulation develops patience in us; and patience, experience; and experience, hope, "And hope maketh not ashamed." Our model for faith is Abraham, who in a very this-worldly concern, the hope for an heir in the Lord, "against all hope believed in hope" (Rom. 4:18), and for this reason became the father of many nations and our model for faith.

It is very necessary and important to emphasize the fact of hope in the Christian's life and outlook. Too many churchmen today act as though any hope within history is a betrayal of faith! Recently, a book was published in the United States whose author was, as an unbeliever, high up in the circles of political power. He fell from this eminence into prison, where he was converted. After his conversion, one providential blessing after another came his way, and yet, in a 1987 book, he treats hope as utopianism and an evidence of bad faith! He apparently believes that having no hope for our future in this world is proof of faith! In 1985, at a church con-

2. Brooke Foss Westcott, *St. Paul's Epistle to the Ephesians* (Grand Rapids, MI: Eerdmans, [1906) 1952), 35-36.

ference, a prominent Christian businessman with a record of dominion in his field, spent his hour of speaking attacking any belief in victory in time and history as a false and unchristian hope. One college student commented: he thinks it was well and good for him to succeed and make his millions, but it's a sin for us to try to do the same!

Paul does not tell us that Jesus Christ *may* be king over the world some day, but rather that he "*is* the blessed and only Potentate, the King of kings, and Lord of lords" (1 Tim. 6:15). John tells us that, as we see the judgments on the nations throughout history, we are to rejoice, because "The kingdoms of this world are become the kingdoms of our Lord, and of his Christ, and he shall reign for ever and ever" (Rev. 11:15). There are many remarkable prophecies, like Isaiah 19:18,

> In that day shall five cities in the land of Egypt speak the language of Canaan, and swear to the LORD of hosts; one shall be called, The city of destruction.

The reference in this prophecy is to this world: there is still enmity to the Lord, but even in Egypt, the type (symbol) of warfare against God and His covenant people, only one city out of six will be outside the faith.

To be without hope is to deny the faith, and to misread Scripture. It is also a lack of knowledge concerning God and His mercy. Two statements in the law are most marvelous in this context:

> 4. Thou shalt not make unto thee any graven image, or any likeness of any thing that is in heaven above, or that is in the earth beneath, or that is in the water under the earth:
> 5. Thou shalt not bow down thyself to them, nor serve them: for I the LORD thy God am a jealous God, visiting the iniquity of the fathers upon the children unto the third and fourth generation of them that hate me. (Ex. 20:4–5)

> 7. The LORD did not set his love upon you, nor choose you, because ye were more in number than any people; for ye were the fewest of all people:

> 8. But because the LORD loved you, and because he would keep the oath which he had sworn unto your fathers, hath the LORD brought you out with a mighty hand, and redeemed you out of the house of bondmen, from the hand of Pharaoh king of Egypt.
> 9. Know therefore that the LORD thy God, he is God, the faithful God, which keepeth covenant and mercy with them that love him and keep his commandments to a thousand generations. (Deut. 7:7–9)

These two texts make two compelling statements, *first*, with respect to God's wrath and judgment, and, *second*, with respect to His grace and mercy. *Both* texts presuppose erring peoples, in the first cases, the fathers; in the second case, the sons. The *sins* of the fathers are visited upon the children to the third and fourth generations. Sin has consequences which are not quickly erased. The consequences of the forest fires in the California mountains of 1987 will not be wiped out in a year or two; recovery will take fifty to one hundred years. The same is true, our text tells us, in the moral realm.

On the other hand, when a people are faithful to God's covenant, however their descendants may sin *and* be judged, God will remember them in judgment and be merciful to a thousand generations of those who are the seed of "them that love Him and keep His commandments." With such a ratio between judgment and mercy, how dare we be without hope?

How true this is we see in an amazing episode in history. In Jeremiah's day, God's Sabbaths for the land were not observed; the laws concerning debt, and release from debt in the Sabbath year were disregarded, and Hebrews who became bondservants because of debt were not released in the Sabbath year but held in slavery. When Nebuchadnezzar marched against Judah, God declared through Jeremiah that they should submit to him, and that they would then survive (Jer. 27:6–18). The nation chose to resist. As the armies approached, and the end seemed near, the people "got religion." They entered into a solemn covenant to obey all of God's law, and, as a preliminary step, freed all the Hebrew slaves they were illegally holding. Then, suddenly, Nebuchadnezzar raised the siege and left. The Judeans demonstrated the superficiality of their recent revival immediately: they reestablished slavery and seized all the bondservants whom they had recently freed. God then declared that He was recalling the army of Nebuchadnezzar to destroy the people and the nation (Jer. 34:8–22).

This is a remarkable episode, an amazing witness to God's mercy. There are times when God says He will not hear a people's prayers (1 Sam. 8:18), and yet He amazes us by His willingness to hear even the prayer of an ungodly man like King Ahab (1 Kings 21:27–29).

It follows clearly that we dare not be without hope, no matter how fearful the world crisis and our plight. In Psalm 46, we have a celebration of the presence and power of God in a time of war, earthquakes, and flood, at a time when men and natural forces alike threatened to wipe out God's people. With them we must say

> 1. God is our refuge and strength, a very present help in trouble.
> 2. Therefore will not we fear, though the earth be removed, and though the mountains be carried into the midst of the sea;
> 3. Though the waters thereof roar and be troubled, though the mountains shake with the swelling thereof. Selah.
> 4. There is a river, the streams whereof shall make glad the city of God, the holy place of the tabernacles of the most High.
> 5. God is in the midst of her; she shall not be moved: God shall help her, and that right early.
> 6. The heathen raged, the kingdoms were moved: he uttered his voice, the earth melted.
> 7. The LORD of hosts is with us; the God of Jacob is our refuge. Selah.
> 8. Come, behold the works of the LORD, what desolations he hath made in the earth.
> 9. He maketh wars to cease unto the ends of the earth; he

> breaketh the bow, and cutteth the spear in sunder; he burneth the chariot in the fire.
> 10. Be still, and know that I am God: I will be exalted among the heathen, I will be exalted in the earth.
> 11. The LORD of hosts is with us; the God of Jacob is our refuge. Selah. (Psalm 46:1–11)

Our God is He who made heaven and earth, and all things therein. He sent His plagues on Egypt and destroyed the power of Pharaoh; He parted the Red Sea asunder and delivered Israel out of Egypt to give them the Promised Land. He raised up kings and prophets, and He humbled nations in terms of His holy purpose. He raised up Jesus Christ from the dead, and performed miracles and raised the dead through His Son and His servants, the apostles.

This is our God, and He has not grown old, nor His arm grown short: He is still in the resurrection business. The ages have not made Him impotent nor weak.

There is no "problem" with God and His power. The problem is with us. Have we become trumpets that sound retreat and defeat, or do we know "the power of His resurrection and the fellowship of His sufferings" (Phil. 3:10), which is the way to triumph?

In the United States, in the 1960s, a popular song with the left, was "We Shall Overcome." But only Christians are truly overcomers, and only so when they live by faith, hope, and love, and obediently so. As John tells us:

> 1. Whosoever believeth that Jesus is the Christ is born of God: and every one that loveth him that begat loveth him also that is begotten of him.
> 2. By this we know that we love the children of God, when we love God, and keep his commandments.
> 3. For this is the love of God, that we keep his commandments: and his commandments are not grievous.
> 4. For whatsoever is born of God overcometh the world: and this is the victory that overcometh the world, even our faith. (1 John 5:1–4)

TEN

The Community of Christ

In 1 John 5:1–5, we are told a number of things of very great importance. Those of concern to us now are, *first,* that all who are born of God "loveth him also that is begotten of him," i.e., our fellow Christians. We are born again into the family of God, and our ties of love must be to that family. *Second,* if we love God, we "keep his commandments." These commandments include many laws concerning our neighbor. In the parable of judgment, our Lord confronts many who call Him "Lord," but to whom he says,

> 41. ... Depart from me, ye cursed, into everlasting fire, prepared for the devil and his angels:
> 42. For I was an hungred, and ye gave me no meat: I was thirsty, and ye gave me no drink:
> 43. I was a stranger, and ye took me not in: naked, and ye clothed me not: sick, and in prison, and ye visited me not.
> 44. Then shall they also answer him, saying, Lord, when saw we thee an hungred, or athirst, or a stranger, or naked, or sick, or in prison, and did not minister unto thee?

> 45. Then shall he answer them, saying, Verily I say unto you, Inasmuch as ye did it not to one of the least of these, ye did it not to me. (Matt. 25:41–45)

Paul tells us, "we are members one of another" (Eph. 4:25). Very clearly, the Lord takes this very literally and seriously as our relationship one to another in Him. We must obey His law, "and his commandments are not grievous" (1 John 5:3). *Third,* when we live in this faithfulness, we are a people whose faith overcomes the world. As we love one another in obedience to God's law, we have a victory over the world because we are bringing every realm into captivity to Christ our Lord. *Fourth,* it is clear that what John means by "believing" is not easy believism but faith with works, faith in action in Christ's name and power (James 2:12–26).

What can be done to become members one of another? What follows is simply a survey of some major applications of this duty by various churches.

First, about ten years ago, one newly organized congregation faced the problem of the need of many members, young and old. Many faced crises for which they had insufficient money to meet unexpected problems. The deacons set up an interest-free loan fund, in terms of Scripture (Lev. 25:35–38), for all such members. If, in six years, the persons were unable to pay, the debt was cancelled. Since its inception, this loan fund has grown; grateful borrowers have often added to it when able, and other members contribute regularly in order to contain all financial crises within the church community. The church has not been without its serious problems and crises, but it has weathered them and grown stronger because they are a community, members one of another, a family in Christ. They have grown, and some satellite congregations have been formed under the leadership of Pastor Joseph C. Morecraft, III.

The notable—and sad—fact is that this practice is a rare one, even though it is clearly required by Scripture. The members are freed from the heavy toll of usury or interest; they are not only loaned money, but they are given the variety of practical helps their circumstances require. Even more, when they face their problem, they have not only the interest-free loan but the prayers of their fellow members.

Many churches and Christian groups, *second*, under the leadership of lawyer Laurence Eck, have established courts of reconciliation. This is in obedience to 1 Corinthians 6:1ff., wherein Paul orders the church to set up its own courts and administer justice in terms of God's law. The early church established such courts with great success; even the pagans resorted to them, knowing their reputation for justice. For centuries, these courts were basic to the life of Europe.

Today these courts are more and more in evidence in the United States. The law of 1 Corinthians 6 reflects the Old Testament law, and rabbinical courts as they function in the United States still settle cases. Such courts, Jewish and Christian, often settle cases among others than their group. In 1968, Black and Puerto Rican tenants in Boston, Massachusetts, took their landlords to court. Their buildings were unsafe and rat-infested; they also accused the landlords of rent gouging. The landlords said the tenants were destructive of property and derelict in paying. The case was settled by a rabbinical court, one originating in Exodus 19 and Deuteronomy 1, and it found both parties at fault. Both sides faced up to their failures. The landlords provided repairs, janitorial service, periodic painting, and adequate utilities. The tenants agreed to assume responsibilities for the care of their own premises.[1]

Across the United States, all kinds of cases are being regularly settled by Christian courts. Both sides sign a contract agreeing to abide by the decision. The goal is not only to settle the legal dispute but also to affect a godly reconciliation between the opposing parties.

Third, a few years ago, John Whitehead, a Christian attorney, profoundly influenced by Samuel Rutherford's *Lex*

---

1. Lynn R. Buzzard and Laurence Eck, *Tell it to the Church* (Wheaton, IL: Tyndale House, 1985), 88-89.

Rex, started the Rutherford Institute. Its work is to defend Christians in court, i.e., persecuted Christian schools, home-schools, or parents; churches; anti-abortion groups, and so on. Today there are member chapters of the Institute in many states, and their record of court victories is a very fine one. They are still far from being able to take on all cases, but their case load is an impressive one, and their legal work has gained them the respectful attention of non-Christian groups and publications.

The Rutherford Institute does *not* believe that our Christian call is to defeat but to victory: "this is the victory that overcometh the world, even our faith" (1 John 5:4). Not too long ago, an atheist who was being denied a civil liberty, appealed to the Rutherford Institute, and they successfully defended him. They maintain a strongly Christian restraint and charity towards all groups. Here again, one man's vision has created a national organization. Both Eck and Whitehead were materially more prosperous before assuming their present callings, but they have embarked on tasks of Christian reconstruction in faith.

Fourth, a great many churches have started ministries to the sick and the aged. A few larger churches hire a visiting nurse to call on those in the church who need their services. In most cases, the women of the church organize visitation groups to take turns helping in all such cases. This may involve nursing care, house cleaning, taking the elderly shopping if the stores are not nearby, and so on and on. Visits to nursing homes are also made.

Among other such services, in some cases young mothers who are ailing and over-burdened are also assisted.

The premise is that needs in the body of Christ must be met.

Fifth, many churches and Christian organizations collect clothing which cannot be sold from stores to be distributed to the poor. Damaged but still good cartons and cans of food are also collected from wholesale houses for distribution. One church, itself made up of the poor, managed to raise funds to buy an old, long unused hotel as a shelter for homeless street people. The two young pastors of this church, both Black, James C. Gilmer and Fred A. Judy, were converted while in the Navy, and they returned to a port city to begin a remarkable ministry which includes a Christian school, a ministry to the needy and to the homeless, and more.

Sixth, there are at least one hundred ministries to delinquent children and youth. The late Rev. Lester Roloff established several homes for such youths, some coming out of drug trafficking, prostitution, theft, and even crimes like murder. Despite their persecution by state authorities, such works of ministry like Roloff's continue.

Seventh, there are many prison ministries; *eighth,* ministries to drug addicts; *ninth,* rescue missions in urban areas and more.

Much more can be said. Homeschooling and Christian schools in the United States now may have as much as thirty-five percent of the school population. A variety of other ministries also exist.

The church at one time had a total vision and ministry, but, in the modern age, it has surrendered its ancient works of mercy to a cold state bureaucracy. In 1890, a remarkable book was written summoning Christians to save the lost and to remake their lives and all society in terms of Christ's mandate to seek and to save the lost. That book was General William Booth's *In Darkest England and the Way Out.* Booth said, of the drunkards, the prostitutes, and the hoodlums he knew,

> For thousands upon thousands of these poor wretches are, as Bishop South truly said, "not so much born into this world as damned into it." The bastard of a harlot, born in a brothel, suckled on gin, and familiar from earliest infancy with all the bestialities of debauch, violated before she is twelve, and driven out into the streets by her mother a year or two later, what chance is there for such a girl in this world—I say nothing about the next? Yet such a case is not

> exceptional. There are many such differing in detail, but in essentials the same. And with boys it is almost as bad. There are thousands who are begotten when both parents were besotted with drink, whose mothers saturated themselves with alcohol every day of their pregnancy, who may be said to have sucked in a taste for strong drink with their mothers' milk, and who were surrounded from childhood with opportunities and incitements to drink. How can we marvel that the constitution thus disposed to intemperance finds the stimulus of drink indispensable? Even if they make a stand against it, the increasing pressure of exhaustion and of scanty food drives them back to the cup. Of these poor wretches, born slaves of the bottle, predestined to drunkenness from their mother's womb, there are—who can say how many? ... if any social scheme is to be comprehensive and practical it must deal with these men. It must provide for the drunkard and the harlot as it provides for the improvident and the out-of-work. But who is sufficient for these things?[2]

Booth called for strong efforts to save these lost, to place them in rescue homes, in Christian job training centers, and so on. He also wanted to set up poor man's banks, and to provide poor man's lawyers. He wanted to revive the doctrine of Christians as a family and a community and wrote:

> ...There is not one sinner in the world—no matter how degraded and dirty he may be—whom my people will not rejoice to take by the hand and pray with, and labour for, if thereby they can but snatch him as a brand from the burning. Now we want to make more use of this, to make the Salvation Army the nucleus of a great agency for bringing comfort and counsel to those who are at their wits' end, feeling as if in the whole world there was no one to whom they could go.

---

2. General William Booth, *In Darkest England and the Way Out* (New York, NY: Funk & Wagnalls, 1890), 47.

> What we want to do is to exemplify to the world the family idea. "Our Father" is the keynote. One is Our Father, then all we are brethren.[3]

Booth wanted to overcome an evil he saw in the churches: he said they mummified their converts so that they were capable of little more than sitting in a church pew. He did *not* expect all believers to join him in the streets, but he did expect all to be active in their faith and strongly supportive of all ministries of grace and mercy. He found evil in the rigidity of Christian institutions, declaring:

> There is a story told likely enough to be true about a young girl who applied one evening for admission to some home established for the purpose of rescuing fallen women. The matron naturally inquired whether she had forfeited her virtue; the girl replied in the negative. She had been kept from that infamy, but she was poor and friendless, and wanted somewhere to lay her head until she could secure work, and obtain a home. The matron must have pitied her, but she could not help her as she did not belong to the class for whose benefit the Institution was intended. The girl pleaded, but the matron could not alter the rule, and dare not break it, they were so pressed to find room for their own poor unfortunates, and she could not receive her. The poor girl left the door reluctantly but returned in a very short time, and said, "I *am* fallen now, will you take me in?"
>
> I am somewhat slow to credit this incident; anyway it is true in spirit, and illustrates the fact that while there are homes to which any poor, ruined, degraded harlot can run for shelter, there is only here and there a corner to which a poor friendless, moneyless, homeless, but unfallen girl can fly for shelter from the storm which bids fair to sweep her away whether she will or no into the deadly vortex of ruin which gapes beneath her.[4]

---

3. Ibid., 218-19.
4. Ibid., 192.

Thus, Booth had in mind the needs of all kinds of peoples, a total ministry in Christ's name.

At this distance in time, it is hard for us to appreciate the hostility Booth's book aroused from Christians and non-Christians. All kinds of reasons were given as to why what he wrote about *was not needed.*[5] The real reason, however, was not stated: they refused to be members of one another. Will we also refuse?

---

5. St. John Ervine, *God's Soldier, General William Booth,* Vol. 2 (New York, NY: Macmillan, 1935), 702-734.

ELEVEN

Christianity and Culture, Part 1

One of the great evils of our time is the false view of culture. In the Soviet Union, with its horrors of slave labor camps, torture, and oppressive tyranny, culture is very proudly cultivated. Every city of any size has what is called a culture center where performances of ostensible art are to be seen. By parading touring ballet groups, and various musicians, throughout the West, the Soviet Union seeks to promote itself as a center of culture. Culture for them as for many in the West is associated with the arts. Is this valid? Does the theater represent culture?

When we turn to the experts, we find even less direction. The *Dictionary of Anthropology* tells us:

> Culture. All that which is nonbiological and socially transmitted in a society, including artistic, social, ideological, and religious patterns of behavior, and the techniques for mastering the environment.[1]

---

1. Charles Winick, *Dictionary of Anthropology* (New York, NY: Philosophical Library, 1956), 144.

The *Dictionary of Sociology* is similar and more precise:

> Culture. A collective name for all behavior patterns socially acquired and socially transmitted by means of symbols; hence a name for all the distinctive achievements of human groups, including not only such items as language, tool-making, industry, art, science, law, government, morals, and religion, but also the material instruments or artifacts in which cultural achievements are embodied and by which intellectual cultural features are given practical effect, such as buildings, tools, machines, communication devices, art objects, etc...[2]

This definition goes on to include all languages, traditions, customs, and institutions within the definition. Both of these dictionary definitions seek to be scientifically precise, but both are essentially meaningless because they are so general and lacking in focus. A lack of focus means a blurred picture. These definitions seek to be precise and all-inclusive. Scientists, as they study "native cultures," seek to collect every kind of available data in order to understand the culture, and one such form of data is *religious.* However, as Henry R. Van Til observed some years ago,

> Culture, however, does not include religion. The notion that it does is the basic error of practically all our cultural anthropologists, which fact may be ascertained by perusing casually any standard work on anthropology by such authors as Van der Leeuw, Malinowsky, and others. Also, Matthew Arnold gives the impression that culture is more inclusive than religion. But the basic assumption underlying this position negates Christianity and is thoroughly naturalistic.[3]

Van Til shows that culture does not include religion, because *culture is religion externalized.* All things in a society have their focus in terms of the faith of a society. The religious focus of the

---

2. Charles A. Ellwood, "Culture," in Henry Pratt Fairchild, editor, *Dictionary of Sociology* (New York, NY: Philosophical Library, 1944), 80.

3. Henry R. Van Til, *The Calvinistic Concept of Culture* (Philadelphia, PA: The Presbyterian and Reformed Publishing Co., 1959), 27.

modern world is humanistic, and hence men and nations externalize their humanistic faith in all that they do.

This at once confronts us with our problem. Since culture is religion externalized, what has happened to Christianity? If we step into the street, we see the culture of humanism all around us. If we pick up a newspaper, or turn on the television set, again we see the culture of humanism. We live in a very intensely religious time, and the religion of our day is humanism, *the worship of man.* Rightly or wrongly, at one time religious dissent with the established forms of Christianity was forbidden. *Now,* it is strictly forbidden, and often punishable by law, to cite the faults and crimes of any minority group, however true our facts may be. The equal rights of all men are seen now as the true gospel, and none had better challenge that faith. We see humanism externalized all around us. Our laws are increasingly humanistic, and, even worse, our churches are also. It does no good and in some countries much evil if there is an established church and that church is humanistic. In Sweden, all citizens vote in the elections of church boards, and atheists and Marxists regularly dominate the churches. In one form or another, humanism is the established religion of most nations. The old forms of the Christian establishment may remain, but the substance is gone.

It can be argued that many churches are evangelical, and therefore the situation is not as bad as it seems. Let us go back to our definition of culture as *religion externalized.* Beginning with the movement known as Pietism, Christianity has steadily *internalized.* It would be absurd to conclude from the statements of the Pietists that a warm, vital religious experience was previously lacking in either Catholic or Protestant circles. The idea has no historical substance. The reformers on the continent, and in England and Scotland, were men of great and passionate faith. How trivial such a downgrading of these men can be I saw in one pastor, who insisted that John Calvin was an unsaved man, because nowhere in his writings does he witness to his conversion experience! I told the man that Calvin believed it to be more important to proclaim the word of God than his own experience. This is the key. Among the followers of Zinzendorf, a founder of the movement, it was held to be more important to read the sermons of the *Ordinaries* than to study the Bible directly.[4] Pietism *resented* sound and substantial thinking and preaching and preferred emotionalism to doctrine. The preoccupation of the reformers with the glory of God and the Kingdom of God was replaced by emphasis on the salvation of man and man's experience.[5]

In terms of Scripture, man's salvation is the starting point, not the goal. Our Lord declares, "Seek ye first the Kingdom of God, and His righteousness" (or justice), *not* our glorious experience (Matt. 6:33).

Pietism internalized religion and warred against the externalization of Christianity. In the United States, Pietism was against Christian schools; it withdrew from a multitude of charitable ministries to concentrate on two things: *first,* soul-saving in terms of a man-centered emphasis; and, *second,* many spiritual retreats and conferences designed to build up the devotional life and joy of one and all rather than to stimulate Christian ministries of compassion and mercy. With the rise of Pietism, talk of love abounded, and the practices decreased.

An illustration will indicate the results of all of this. John Lofton, of the Chalcedon staff, criticized in a newspaper article the lack of a *Christian* concern by Mrs. Nancy Reagan, and by her staff, with respect to a particular issue. A member of the staff called to challenge Lofton's statement, and she identified herself as a Christian. John asked, then why haven't I seen any evidence of this? Her answer was that her faith was a very precious and private matter. John's response was, how can it be Christian if it is so private? Shortly thereafter, a very prominent and close associate of President Reagan called to rebuke John Lofton for "dragging in" Christianity to a polit-

---

4. F. Ernest Stoeffler, *German Pietism During the Eighteenth Century* (Leiden, Netherlands: E. J. Brill, 1973), 161.

5. F. Ernest Stoeffler, *The Rise of Evangelical Pietism* (Leiden, Netherlands: E. J. Brill, 1971), 55.

ical commentary; he added that he was a Christian and was counseling John as a Christian! John Lofton, on a first name basis with this man, answered, "I've known you for many years and never guessed you were a Christian. Where do you keep your faith, in a closet?" A grim sequel to this episode is the fact that within a year or so, this presidential aide was under indictment for dishonesty.

How can Christianity have an impact on our culture if it is held to be a private matter? How can a faith be vital if it is limited to emotional experiences and not a matter of life and action? If we are the salt of the earth, as our Lord requires us to be, it means that we are the preserving agent of the world. Without us, the world would plunge into total corruption. Salt that is worthless is not thrown into the garden, lest it kill the plants. It is thrown into the path, "to be trodden under foot of men" (Matt. 5:13). This is how the Lord judges a church which fails to do its work. Similarly, we are called to be the light of the world, to be the cultural and life force. It is an active faith which the Lord requires of us: "Let your light so shine before men, *that they may see your good works,* and glorify your Father which is in heaven" (Matt. 5:16). This tells us three things. *First,* we are to be the transmitters of the light of God's wisdom, Jesus Christ, to all men. *Second,* they must see our "good works," our obedience to every word that proceeds out of the mouth of God (Matt. 4:4). Our Lord's statement to Satan comes from Deuteronomy 8:1–3:

> 1. All the commandments which I command thee this day shall ye observe to do, that ye may live, and multiply, and go in and possess the land which the LORD sware unto your fathers.
> 2. And thou shalt remember all the way which the LORD thy God led thee these forty years in the wilderness, to humble thee, and to prove thee, to know what was in thine heart, whether thou wouldest keep his commandments, or no.
> 3. And he humbled thee, and suffered thee to hunger, and fed thee with manna, which thou knewest not, neither did

> thy fathers know: that he might make thee know that man doth not live by bread only, but by every word that proceedeth out of the mouth of the Lord doth man live.

Our Lord declares that He lives by the law of God, not by the law of Satan as set forth in Genesis 3:5, whereby man makes himself his own god, knowing, or determining for himself, what is good and evil, what is law and morality, and the way that he should go. *Third*, men will glorify our Father in heaven when they see us live in this kind of faithfulness. The culture of our world will then be Christian, because culture is religion externalized to govern every area of life and thought.

The dictionary definitions of culture cited early were wrong in that they denied the religious focus of culture. They were right in seeing every area of life and thought, including language, as an aspect of culture. (Western languages reflect deeply the imprint of the Bible.) They were wrong in failing to recognize that it is *religion* which shapes a culture. But how could they know this when most Christians fail to recognize it? If we do not provide the light, who will?

TWELVE

Christianity and Culture, Part 2

Our Lord commands us in the Sermon on the Mount to be the light of the world (Matt. 5:16). David declares of God,

> For with thee is the fountain of life: in thy light shall we see light. (Psalm 36:9)

But men seek light elsewhere; rather, they seek to be their own light. Isaiah tells us of God's verdict on all such men:

> Behold, all ye that kindle a fire, that compass yourselves about with sparks: walk in the light of your fire, and in the sparks that ye have kindled. This shall ye have of mine hand; ye shall lie down in sorrow. (Isaiah 50:11)

Rather than the light of God, men seek to generate their own light and vision. They are men of darkness, seeking an escape by their own self-exaltation. They dream that their wisdom will give them the necessary light. Calvin felt that God was saying to all such men, You have rejected Me and sought to kindle your own light to escape the darkness. Well, now your life will take its course in your own fire, which will be, not your salvation, but your destruction: "at the place of torment ye shall lie down!"[1] They will create the culture of death.

We have seen that the false definition of culture restricts it to an upper class element interested in the arts. This interest is a non-Christian and therefore a superficial one. In New York, people read, not books so much as book reviews, to know how to think; they visit the "trendy" art galleries in order to know art as it presently is supposed to be. The "legitimate theater" may be offering garbage, even as the films and television do, but it is "high" art as against the "low-brow" art of the more popular media. In a meaning unintended by Alan Levy in *The Culture Vultures* (1968), these people, whether in New York, London, Paris, or Moscow, are culture vultures.

Culture vultures believe that only the best in art is true culture, and it is to be enjoyed only by the best among men, namely, themselves. The popular definitions of culture are thus elitist as well as anti-Christian. In this sense, culture is seen as the prerogative of an exclusive group of people to the exclusion of those deemed uncultured.

Our Lord, however, sees the necessity of externalizing the new life we have in Him. Because we are regenerated by His saving grace, we must seek to regenerate all men and to work for the "new heavens and a new earth, wherein dwelleth righteousness" (2 Peter 3:13). We are the people of the Jubilee, and our Lord at Nazareth read the great Jubilee proclamation of Isaiah 61:1ff.:

> 16. And he came to Nazareth, where he had been brought up: and, as his custom was, he went into the synagogue on the Sabbath day, and stood up for to read.
> 17. And there was delivered unto him the book of the prophet Esaias. And when he had opened the book, he found the place where it was written,
> 18. The Spirit of the Lord is upon me, because he hath anointed me to preach the gospel to the poor; he hath sent

---

1. Edward J. Young, *The Book of Isaiah*, Vol. 3 (Grand Rapids, MI: Eerdmans, 1972), 304-05.

> me to heal the brokenhearted, to preach deliverance to the captives, and recovering of sight to the blind, to set at liberty them that are bruised.
> 19. To preach the acceptable year of the Lord.
> 20. And he closed the book, and he gave it again to the minister, and sat down. And the eyes of all them that were in the synagogue were fastened on him
> 21. And he began to say unto them, This day is this scripture fulfilled in your ears. (Luke 4:16–21)

These verses were part of the early church's marching orders. They preached salvation through the atoning sacrifice of Jesus Christ. They had a ministry of healing, and they soon established hospitals. They preached to the poor as well as the rich; they healed the brokenhearted, ransomed captives, healed the spiritually as well as the physically blind, and they set free the oppressed, those bruised or crushed by oppression.

The early church included many prominent people, lawyers, philosophers, men of state, and so on. But it also included slaves, and the poor. Such a mingling of peoples in an elitist culture brought them contempt as a slave religion. These despised Christians were creating a Christian culture, one in which all relations, vocations, spheres of activity, and persons were aspects of God's Kingdom and an evidence of a new culture. The Christians were hated because they were effectual and successful.

This hatred is a witness to Christian power. John Dryden in the seventeenth century showed aristocratic disdain for the Puritans as trash, describing them as the "rascal rabble …whom kings no title gave, and God no grace."[2] This same "cultured contempt" is very much with us still.

One index to our loss of cultural power is the fact that a once very important Christian doctrine is now rarely heard of, namely, *providence.* The Westminster Larger Catechism tells us,

2. Ruth Nevo, *The Dial of Virtue, A Study of Poems on Affairs of State in the Seventeenth Century* (Princeton, NJ: Princeton, University Press, 1963), 254.

> 18. God's works of providence are his most holy, wise, and powerful preserving, and governing all his creatures; ordering them, and all their actions, to his own glory.

It was held also that, because man is created in God's image, man therefore has a duty to be *provident.* For this reason, over the centuries, the provident duties were faithfully preached and practiced: family virtues, thrift, charity, work, honesty, a trustworthy word, and so on. The Puritans especially stressed these things and thereby became powerful. Providence was a favorite doctrine for them, and a name given to ships and to at least one city. Providence, Charity, Faith, Hope, and like names were commonly given to girls.

In the past two hundred years, Providence has been steadily replaced by Revolution. Instead of stressing providence, the culture of Revolution stresses envy and violence. The work ethic has been replaced by the envy ethic. The solution to problems is not God's law faithfully observed but the violent overthrow of the present order. The doctrine of Providence stresses the ultimate harmony of all interests in the Lord, whereas Revolution insists on the continual conflict of interests. As early as 1659 in England, men were turning from Providence to Revolution. Richard Flecknoe wrote, "all things in this world being in perpetual revolution, tis impossible from the beginning to see the end of all things."[3] The believers in God's providence held and hold with Peter, "Known unto God are all his works from the beginning of the world" (Acts 15:18). Moreover, God sets forth His work in His word, so that it is possible from the beginning to see the end of all things.

It is God's providence that all manner of men be saved, that all peoples, tribes, tongues, and nations know Christ as Lord and Savior (Rev. 5:9).

This cannot be done if we are poor towards God and His servants. In the eighteenth century, an evil idea gained power which in many circles is still with us. In Scotland, the General

3. Ibid., 95.

Assembly, with lay leaders dominating it, refused to raise ministerial salaries. Their self-righteous and hypocritical argument was this: "A poor church is a pure church." The result was the triumph of secularism.[4]

According to Jeffrey Burton Russell, basic to medieval culture was the fact that "holiness, rather than fame or wealth, was the way to obtain status."[5] Without narrowing our vision to holiness, but including godly knowledge and dominion, with righteousness or justice, we must say that a Christian culture must manifest all these things in the service of God, and, in the Lord, to men.

The Greek doctrine of justice was plainly stated by Antiphon the Sophist, apparently an Athenian of the latter half of the fifth century B.C. He declared, "Justice, then, is not to transgress that which is the law of the city in which one is a citizen."[6] This is clear and obvious humanism. It is the faith of our time, and the culture of our time. Righteousness or justice is the tie that binds and holds a culture together. The growing injustice of humanistic states is leading to fearfulness, fragmentation, and inner decay. We must have a Christian culture, governed by God's law-word, and ever mindful that God holds us accountable for the maintenance of His order. The tests of a culture as God declares them are blunt and earnest:

> 21. Thou shalt neither vex a stranger, nor oppress him: for ye were strangers in the land of Egypt.
> 22. Ye shall not afflict any widow, or fatherless child.
> 23. If thou afflict them in any wise, and they cry at all unto me, I will surely hear their cry;
> 24. And my wrath shall wax hot, and I will kill you with the sword; and your wives shall be widows, and your children fatherless. (Ex. 22:21–24)

---

4. G. R. Cragg, *The Church and the Age of Reason, 1648-1789* (Grand Rapids, MI: Eerdmans, [1962] 1967), 91.

5. Jeffrey Burton Russell, *A History of Medieval Christianity, Prophecy and Order* (New York, NY: Thomas Y. Crowell, 1968), 84.

6. Kathleen Freeman, *Ancilla to the Pre-Socratic Philosophers* (Cambridge, MA: Harvard University Press, 1957), 147.

A Christian culture begins where other cultures do not venture, with the word of God and His mandate to us for every sphere of life and thought.

THIRTEEN

The Will to Autonomy

Modern culture is radically anti-Christian and is a development of the premises of Genesis 3:5, man's desire to be his own god, knowing or determining good and evil for himself. This means a will to autonomy and aseity. *Autonomy* means self-law, i.e., being governed by no law other than the law of one's being. *Aseity* means self-being, to be god, uncreated and totally independent of all other creatures and things.

In practice, this will to autonomy can have various manifestations. It can mean asceticism as a denial of human needs, i.e., for food, sex, fellowship, and more. It can also mean a contempt for such things by excess, i.e., musical chairs sex as performed by some Eastern mystics to show that sex means nothing and is performed as a trifling and meaningless act. Both attitudes are very much with us.

Some years ago, a young woman came to hear me two or three times, not out of any interest in what I had to say but because someone had told her I brought "common sense" helpfulness to problems. She subsequently sought my counsel. She and her husband were notable in society and were sometimes in society news photographs. He was tall, athletic, handsome, and blond; she had light brown hair, was also tall and very beautiful. Her problem was this: she was an excellent homemaker, an outstanding cook, and a sexually desirable woman, yet her husband belittled all her accomplishments, had sexual relations with her at most once a month, and yet was not adulterous, nor was she. She had the virginal quality of one who had never involved herself in anything good or evil and had known life only on the surface. She was deeply hurt and shaken by her husband's attitude. What came out was simply this: he was fully aware of her qualities; he found her very desirable sexually; he had married her because possession of her was a major social asset and triumph *but* he resented needing her and desiring her sexually. He found marital sex degrading because it made clear his physical dependence on her, and therefore he felt "less than human." For him, to be a free man meant to use all things without needing or loving anyone or anything. He saw need and dependency as a surrender of freedom and manhood.

He may have been unaware of existentialist philosophy, but he was in essence an existentialist. Freedom for him meant no ties to the past, nor to the present. It meant self-determination in terms of his own desire for autonomy. Despite his obvious benefits from his parents and their advantages, he was embarrassed around them, because their presence reminded him of his derivative and dependent being. He was a classic case of would-be autonomous man. It pleased him that other men desired his wife and envied him his possession of so sexually desirable a woman, and yet he resented desiring her himself, because it made clear his unwilling dependency.

Sex in our time is very much over-stressed and over-rated as a factor in men's lives. Clearly, the sexual urge can be a strong drive, but the will to be god is far stronger. The lust for autonomy and aseity is the central force in fallen man. One man, later under psychiatric care as a sexual offender, revealed his motivation in a comment to his very much abused wife: "I can do as I please with you, and it means nothing to me and everything to you."

In 1982, the Higher Heights Christian School of Martinez, California began a Community Assistance Program to help feed the hungry of Contra Costa County. By late February, an average of two hundred and forty families each day, four days a week, were being fed. These were truly hungry people, obviously malnourished, and some were too hungry to wait to leave the school building before stuffing the food into their mouths.

All the same, a number of people refused the food when they learned it came from Christians and not the Federal government. Although bureaucratic delays prevented them from receiving the federal aid, they felt that such statist aid was their "right," and they wanted their "rights" rather than Christian help or charity.

This is not an isolated example. Christian help or charity is personal; it establishes a personal relationship from which concern and gratitude flow. At times the persons manning the charity work come from the same social strata as the recipients; the donors know that a change in the economic situation can make them jobless recipients of charity. A Christian bond of grace and concern commonly results. The will to autonomy cannot tolerate such an interdependence.

Statist welfarism thus fits the modern temper. It is impersonal. It is a "right," and it does not offend the pride of man. We read, in one of the Elizabethan homilies,

> And our Saviour Christ saith *there is none good but God*, and that *we can do nothing* that is good *without him*, nor *no man can come to the Father but by him*. He commandeth us all to say that *we be unprofitable servants, when we have done all that we can do*. He preferreth the penitent Publican before the proud, holy, and glorious Pharisee. He calleth himself a *Physician, but not to them that be whole, but to them that be sick*, and have need of his salve for their sore. He teacheth us in our prayers to reknowledge ourselves sinners, and to ask

> forgiveness and deliverance from all evils at our heavenly Father's hand. He declareth that the sins of our own hearts deserveth condemnation, affirming that *we shall give an account for every idle word.* He saith *he came not to save but the sheep that were* utterly *lost* and cast away. Therefore few of the proud, just, learned, wise, perfect, and holy Pharisees were saved by him: because they justified themselves by their counterfeit holiness before men. Wherefore, good people, let us beware of such hypocrisy, vainglory, and justifying of ourselves. Let us look upon our feet and then down peacock's feathers, down proud heart, down vile clay, frail and brittle vessels.[1]

Modern statism seeks in every sphere to objectify and depersonalize essentially personal activities. It creates agencies which ostensibly provide for a variety of services as their logical function and thereby relieve men of personal responsibilities. The problem, however, is that when the citizen relieves himself of responsibilities, the citizen as bureaucrat is no more mindful of them either. Depersonalization sets in everywhere. Not diaconal grace nor personal concern but "social" problems and needs result. No man gains by being either the taxed donor or the anonymous recipient of statist welfare. Responsibility disappears on both sides. The affluent are ready to condemn the degeneracy of the welfare mobs but fail to see the degeneracy of the more or less affluent citizenry, themselves. The corruption and depersonalization of welfarism works both ways. It is an aspect of the modern will to autonomy, and it is more clearly present in the non-recipient than the recipient. For too many of the non-recipients, humanity in any worthwhile sense ends with them.

Impersonal welfarism from the days of Rome to the present creates a *mob.* Basic to the development of a mob is depersonalization. Neither the person nor morality govern or are operative in a mob.

---

1. "A Sermon of the Misery of all Mankind and of his Condemnation to Death Everlasting by his own Sin," from *The Two Books of Homilies Appointed to be Read in Churches* (Oxford, England: Oxford University Press, 1859), 19-20. This sermon is from the First Book of Homilies, July 1547.

Man was created by God to live in community, not autonomy. Man's personhood is a reflection of the personhood or image of God. Man by his sin seeks autonomy, an impossibility, and the negation of his true being. By seeking aseity and autonomy, man gains, not the desired godhood, but a descent into the mob. Failure to be a community in the triune God means a collapse into the anarchy of the mob.

Community is a theological fact, not a statist one.

FOURTEEN

GOVERNMENT AND DOMINION

St. John Chrysostom (c. 347-407 A.D.) is famous for his golden-tongued oratory, and also for his resistance to imperial power. He is less well known for his works of charity. In his day, the Christians at Constantinople numbered c. 100,000. According to J. G. Davies, the Christians "held themselves responsible for the maintenance of fifty thousand poor folk." In addition to the support of the clergy, three thousand widows and virgins were supported. The funds for the varied work of the church came from the tithes and offerings of the faithful; there were also receipts from lands and properties bequeathed to the church, and the emperor gave an allowance to the church. The poor-fund had Chrysostom's especial attention and concern.[1] At the same time, Chrysostom served as a judge, a function assumed early in church history in terms of Paul's command in 1 Corinthians 6:1–6.[2] These hearings were held on Mondays so that peace might be reestablished

1. J. G. Davies, *Daily Life of Early Christians* (New York, NY: Duell, Sloan and Pearce, 1953), 167–68.

2. Ibid., 169–172.

between the contending parties by and after the decision and before the following Sunday.[3]

All this was by no means unusual. Christians took seriously Paul's command that Christians must judge or govern the world (1 Cor. 6:2–3). They early established their own courts of law, schools, welfare work, hospitals, and more.

W. H. C. Frend, in surveying the history of the church to 604 A.D., mentions in passing some of the activities Christians had instituted. Many of these were things common to Jewish life, in obedience to Biblical law. The apocryphal *Book of Tobit* gives us evidence of this. Tobit counsels his son to give alms faithfully, pay all workmen promptly, to eat his bread with the hungry and the needy, and to clothe the naked. "See that those never do to another what thou wouldst hate to have done to thee by another" (Tobit 4:15). The apostate emperor, Julian, recognized that pagans were attracted to Christianity by its community life: "No Jew ever has to beg, and the impious Galileans support not only their own poor but ours as well."[4] Hermas wrote of the Christian duty to care for widows and orphans, to relieve distressed believers, to practice hospitality, to reverence the aged, practice justice, and to preserve their brotherhood. All the early literature stressed such responsibilities.[5] Prisoners seized by raiders were ransomed. The church, like the Jewish synagogue, acted as a trustee for widows and orphans, and Cyprian compared the clergy with the Levites of the Old Testament in their responsibilities.[6] The sick and captives were to be visited; a decent burial for Christian dead was seen as another responsibility.[7] Church buildings were more impressive and better constructed than others, and they included rooms for the storage of provisions for the needy.[8] Basil the Great used monks to staff schools, orphanages, and

---

3. Ibid., 169.

4. W. H. C. Frend, *The Rise of Christianity* (Philadelphia, PA: Fortress Press, 1984), 25.

5. Ibid., 133.

6. Ibid., 404-05.

7. Ibid., 421.

8. Ibid., 558.

hospitals.[9] Pope Gregory I took care not to waste the Lord's assets. Careful records were kept of all those who received charity, how much and on what date. Fraud was emphatically discouraged. Gregory's palace entertained strangers and fed the sick.[10]

The medieval era saw such ministries developed and extended. They continued after the Reformation. In England, the preaching of Thomas Lever (1550) started a major movement to undo the degradations of Henry VIII against the church by making a massive restitution to God by way of Christian works, educational, charitable, and so on.[11] The Church of England's charity schools were a factor in later years.[12]

This very brief survey makes clear that Christians assumed the responsibility for health, education, and welfare. They also provided courts of law to which, in the early centuries, pagans as well as Christians went for justice. *Clearly, the basic government of society was in the hands of Christians, and Christian institutions.*

This should not surprise us. According to Isaiah 9:6, the government shall be on Christ's shoulder. With His coming, His death, resurrection, and ascension, we are told that He "is the blessed and only Potentate, the King of kings, and Lord of lords" (1 Tim. 6:15): *is*, not *shall be.* As kings and priests unto God in Christ (Rev. 1:6), Christians have a duty to rule for Him. We are given this office by virtue of His atonement (Rev. 1:5), so that we are now His dominion people and therefore His justice men, His law defenders.

This faith was not a matter of debate or discussion within the church but a *tacit assumption.* To assume such governmental powers was an affront to the Roman Empire, as it is an affront to the nations today. Marxist states strictly prohibit it; where a pretense of religious freedom is maintained by some,

---

9. Ibid., 631.

10. Ibid., 885.

11. Thomas Lever, *Sermons, 1550* (Westminster, England: Constable, 1901).

12. W. L. Lowther Clarke, *Eighteenth Century Piety* (London, England: Society for Promoting Christian Knowledge, 1944), 45-46., 69ff.

Christians are limited to worship in a few churches, but barred from a governmental and dominion function.

Dominion is the exercise of government, and a religious fact. It was only natural that monks should have first created new lands in the Netherlands with their dikes, cleared forests for farms, and taken rocky and barren areas and converted them into fertile lands. All this and more meant the exercise of dominion, of government in Christ's name.

This governmental mandate was diminished and sometimes extinguished by two things. *First,* within the church, faulty theology, pietism, and antinomianism, and later eschatologies of flight and escapism, led to the collapse of Christian governmental action. *Second,* statism sought to hold exclusive dominion and government in every sphere, and it has successfully gained such powers.

Behind all this have been religious doctrines and movements, humanistic crusades and faiths. In the United States, this anti-Christianity came into focus in Ralph Waldo Emerson, and in Walt Whitman. Whitman's announced purpose, as set forth in "Starting from Paumanok," in the 1892 version, was "Solely to drop in the earth the germs of a greater religion."[13] Whitman saw himself as a poet-prophet, patterning himself after a fictional character in a French novel.[14] In "Chanting the Square Deific" (1865), he presented himself as the current expression of a *pantheistic divinity*:

> Chanting the square deific, out of the One advancing, out of the sides;
> Out of the old and new—out of the square entirely divine,
> Solid, four-sided, (all the sides needed) ... from this side JEHOVAH am I,
> Old Brahm I, and I Saturnius am;
> Not Time affects me—I am Time, old, modern as any,

13. Lawrence I. Buell, "Unitarian Aesthetics and Emerson's Poet Priest," *American Quarterly,* Vol. 20, No. 1, Spring, 1968, 3.

14. Esther Shephard, *Walt Whitman's Pose* (New York, NY: Harcourt, Brace, 1938).

> Unpersuadable, relentless, executing righteous judgments...[15]

In the same "poem," Whitman also identifies himself as Satan.[16] This was not new. In 1855, in "The Sleepers," Whitman declared himself to be "Lucifer's sorrowful terrible heir."[17] What begins as a protest against slavery becomes a "poem" celebrating homosexual fellatio (in section eight).[18] According to Helen Vendler, who admires Whitman, this is compared to the wedding feast at Cana in Galilee, and Christ turning water into wine. (Vendler sees the episode as between Whitman and a virgin.)[19] For our purpose, it is sufficient to say that Whitman, more rigorously than Emerson, not only adopted a new religion but also a new morality. Moreover, for him man's true future was democracy. Whitman's monism, as Rosenstock-Huessy pointed out with respect to all monism, leads to slavery. The only truth for Whitman was the voice of the people, whatever it may say, provided that the people were not Christian. Whitman's writings are a prolonged revolt against Christianity and Christian dominion and government.

Because Whitman's religion is the faith of intellectuals and educators, we have seen the steady advancement of monocratic government by the state. When people today speak of "government," they mean the state, whereas in truth government begins with the self-government of the Christian man, and government means the family, church, school, our vocation, our society and its many institutions and agencies, and only partially the state.

By surrendering dominion and government, churchmen have made themselves irrelevant to God and to man, to heaven and earth alike. Because Christ by His atonement has

---

15. Walt Whitman, *Leaves of Grass* (New York, NY: Grosset & Dunlap, n.d.), 425. The punctuation and capitalizations were altered by Whitman in the so-called deathbed edition of 1892, in which "Jehovah" no longer appears in all capitals, and other adjustments were made.

16. Ibid., 427.

17. Ibid., 98.

18. Ibid., 94.

19. Helen Vendler, "Body Language," in *Harper's Magazine*, Vo. 273, No. 1637, October 1986, 64–65.

made us kings and priests unto God, we have an inescapable duty to exercise dominion and government.

Man is in Christ a prophet, priest, and king. As a prophet, we must each interpret our lives and world in terms of God's law-word and apply that word to every sphere. To be a prophet in Christ is to live by God's every word (Matt. 4:4).

As priests, we dedicate and consecrate ourselves, our world, and our every activity to the triune God. All things must be made holy in Him (Zech. 14:20–21).

As kings, we are to rule the world in Christ and to develop all its potentialities for Him, so that the desert places blossom like the rose (Isa. 35:1).

Our offices in Christ are governmental and dominion callings. We have none other calling in Him.

FIFTEEN

The Problem of Poverty, Part 1

The problem of poverty has been common to all history, but not without very important differences from era to era. *First,* the definitions of what constitute poverty vary. Thus, the modern poor of American cities are "richer" in some respects than successful men of other eras: they usually have hot and cold running water, indoor toilets, better cooking stoves, and more heat than castles once could dream of. The poor in Rome had an experience of deprivation which was much further removed from the wealth of that day than is the gap in our time. *Second,* this tells us that poverty is comparative; the poor of India in the 1980s would regard the poor of New York City as rich. This fact gives us no ground for dismissing the poverty in New York City; it simply tells us that the definition is to a degree relative. The poor in New York commonly have television, something very remote to the poor of Calcutta, but this does not eliminate the fact that the poor in New York see themselves as poor, are seen by their more prosperous New Yorkers as poor, and, in terms of the life of the United States, *are* indeed poor. *Third,* that poverty is relative to a society and its level of prosperity does not eliminate the fact of poverty, nor the very important fact that a gap exists between prosperous Americans and poor Americans, and prosperous Hindus and poor Hindus. In fact, the very existence of the gap between the rich and the poor is an important and central part of *the experience of poverty.* Thus, President Dwight D. Eisenhower described the fact of his family's "poverty" as a child but added, "We never knew we were poor." They were people in a relatively new country enjoying the opportunity to live freely and to advance themselves. Many poor immigrants to the United States have experienced their poverty as new wealth and as a marvelous opportunity.

Fourth, poverty has been politicized in recent years, as it had been in Rome and other civilizations of the past, and this has altered its nature, *because the moral and religious nature of poverty has been lost.* To neglect the theological governance of poverty and wealth is to warp both, to engender a bad conscience, and to foster class hatred.

An early Christian (but *not* Biblical) view of poverty saw it as a blessing. This perspective came into focus in St. Francis of Assisi and very soon thereafter went into decline. It is easy enough to call attention to the neglect of this view by medieval man, of great class differences, and of contempt for the poor, but we must not forget the many wealthy and powerful men who gave their wealth away and assumed a radical poverty for religious reasons. This at times had aspects of a "works" salvation, but it also had genuinely godly grounds and was marked commonly by deep humility. At the same time, the modern rift between the rich and the poor was developing. This modern division is marked by mutual hatred or contempt for the rich or the poor *as a class.* In *Piers Plowman,* a thoroughly medieval work, we see evidences of this modern view. In his "Vision of the Field Full of Folk," we read

> But jesters and janglers, Judas children,
> Feigning their fancies, and fooling the crowds,
> With wit enough to work, if work they would,

> Paul preacheth about them—no more will I say—
> "He that speaketh filthily" is the Devil's man.
> There were tramps and beggars fast about flitting,
> Crammed with bread in wallet and belly,
> Lying for their food, and fighting in the taverns,
> Going to bed in gluttony, rising from bed in ribaldry,
> Gangs of mean thieves.
> Sleep and sorry sloth pursue them ever.[1]

The *accuracy* of Langland's comments about these lower class peoples cannot be doubted, but man must not be viewed in terms merely of what he is, but rather in terms of what God requires of us in His law. Our conduct then is not governed by the fact of man but by the commandments of God. This is not to say that Langland is not aware of this, but simply that the modern view appears in his work also. For example, of the merchants he says:

> Women that bake and brew, butchers and cooks,
> They are the people that harm the poor,
> They harm the poor who can but buy in pennyworths,
> And secretly and oft they poison them;
> They grow rich on their retail with what the poor should eat,
> They buy houses, they become landlords,
> If they sold honestly they would not build so high.[2]

Corruption and adulteration marked the small traders, but Langland saw evil in all groups, high and low, a Christian belief in total depravity. However, this view of sin, without the accompanying belief in God's greater power, in and to all, becomes anti-Christian and dangerous.

What then results is that the rich declare that the poor are poor because they are lazy, improvident, shiftless, immoral, and basically a bad lot. Since all men are sinners, there is truth in this, and it is easy to prove, but it is not the whole truth, and

---

1. Arthur Burrell, editor, *Piers Plowman, The Vision of a People's Christ, by William Langland* (London, England: J. M. Dent, Everyman's Library, [1912] 1925), 4.

2. Ibid., 39-40.

it becomes a lie if these traits are seen as class traits. To restrict evil to a class or race is more than wrong: *it is an evil heresy.*

Even as the rich say these things, they feel guilty! In a meeting of wealthy heirs, only one man, a Christian, stood against a large number of men and women in opposing guilt-ridden grants of money to radical groups as a conscience-salving device. Most men of wealth tend to favor with money groups dedicated to the destruction of wealth! By becoming allies of the anti-capitalist segment of society, such capitalists try to allay their conscience, buy the respect of their enemies, and "earn" the right to continue in their wealth. Their main reward is an increasingly bad conscience, together with a suicidal temper and practice. Throwing money at one's enemies has become a major personal, political, and international practice in the twentieth century, and a major source of troubles.

Moreover, the "solution" of welfarism is divisive of society. The poor often feel they have "rights" simply because they are poor. To view poverty as a condition which gives man rights and entitlements is a strange belief, and a socially destructive one because it rests on envy. Because the rich are rich, the poor because they are poor are "entitled" to a share-the-wealth division of assets and taxes. Welfarism divides society by its impersonalism. The rich look down on the poor as dangerous and mask their fears and self-doubt by dressing up welfarism as love and human concern. Love is not welfarism: if I love someone, I want to be close to them, but welfarism seeks to keep the poor at a distance, a safe and contented distance.

The poor in the welfare state tend to see the rich as exploiters. Instead of seeing wealth as something *produced* by intelligence, work, and capital, they see wealth as a static, unchanging resource which has been expropriated by the rich. As far as the *persons* of the rich are concerned, the poor tend to see them as arrogant, elitist, thoughtless, snobbish, as triflers with other people's lives, and so on. Since *all men* are sinners, it is easy to verify such opinions; there is truth in them, but it is not the whole truth. Each side satisfies itself by damning the other. Class tensions, and even class war, result.

At the same time, like the rich, the poor feel guilty. The wives of the poor often turn on their husbands to indict them as bad because they are poor and are not providing adequately for the family. The poor males often feel that their wives are the nagging culls of womanhood, lusting for rich men. For them, the rich are evil, women are evil, and so too is life.

In a welfare society, class war, race war, and conflict between the sexes is usually close to the surface.

As against welfarism, Christian charity unites rather than divides society. On January 15, 1891, in a sermon at Durham, England, the bishop of Durham, Brooke Foss Westcott, declared in part:

> ...Almsgiving is the natural, the necessary expression of a healthy Christian character. The Christian cannot but be communicative of the goods which he has. Almsgiving is not a concession to importunity, by which we free ourselves from unwelcome petitioners: it is not a sacrifice to public opinion, by which we satisfy the claims popularly made upon our place or fortune: it is not an appeal for praise: it is not a self-complacent show of generosity: it is not, in a word, due to any external motive. It is the spontaneous outcome of life. What the life is, the fruit will be, in the highest forms as in the lowest. Our thoughts have their fruits, and our thoughts themselves are fruits.
>
> In this light we can feel the inexorable truth of the Lord's sentence: *By their fruits ye shall know them.* Nothing can take the place of the ripe results of life. There may be the swift response of a superficial sensibility: there may be the luxuriant growth of lofty intentions: but the blessing is only for him who brings forth fruit—fruit answering to the divine seed—in patience.
>
> The actions of a Christian, then, are a fruit of the Christian character. As we give distinctness to the idea another thought comes out. A real gift is part of ourselves...

> As fruits, therefore, our alms will bear the marks of our Faith…
>
> For the fruit which St. Paul desires for his beloved Philippians is that which aboundeth to their account. The generous deed done in the name of Christ is a fruit, and it is fruitful. *The fruit of the righteous,* in the significant language of Scripture, *is a tree of life.* Each harvest is the seed of still richer return in the time to come. True it is, true beyond all possibility of failure, that 'there can never be one lost good'; and, more than this, the good has in it a power of growth. *One soweth* indeed *and another reapeth,* but they *rejoice together* in the end when their labours are revealed and crowned in life eternal.[3]

When the Biblical view of our *duties* in terms of God's law governs the rich and the poor, they then see their responsibilities in terms of God's law rather than their personal views. It is a sad fact that the poor who prosper are often the least generous to the poor, because they know the poor and go by their knowledge rather than God's law. They see the poor as undeserving too often, and God's law is neglected. The rich can often be as judgmental of their rich neighbor.

Miri Rubin, in studying *Charity and Community in Medieval Cambridge* (1987), saw charity and gifts as important in "social cohesion, peace, and order," and in "forging friendships and alliances." Such charitable giving bound society "closely" in a "network of obligations and expectations." Society, rich and poor together, found itself maintained by "a constant state of debt" in the form of personal ties and obligations. When, later in the medieval era, the religious and theological duty gave way to sociological facts, deep divisions set in. The traditional givers of charity now saw the poor as *outsiders to society,* as people "to be hunted down and put back to work, or into prison" because they were enemies of "social morality."[4]

---

3. Brooke Foss Westcott, *The Incarnation and Common Life* (London, England: Macmillan, 1893), 197-200.

4. Miri Rubin, *Charity and Community in Medieval Cambridge* (Cambridge, England: Cambridge University Press, 1987), 1ff., 10, 32.

Behind the modern sentimentality there is an equally ugly view of the modern poor: they are outsiders to society. Social stratification has set in even within the churches. Churches have in the modern era tended to represent a class group, i.e., upper, middle, or lower, not out of deliberately exclusive policies but because each group or class feels more "comfortable" by itself. In a society extensively governed by envy and class tensions, the various elements do prefer isolation and insularity, and they thereby intensify their differences.

In such a divided society, men are guilt-ridden. Their interracial and interclass associations often are artificial and doctrinaire rather than natural. Guilt governs even their relationship to the earth. Thus, the myth is widely propagated that man has been the major destroyer of plant and animal life. However, out of every one hundred species of flora and fauna known to scientists, ninety-nine died out in remote antiquity. In the past two centuries or so, less than eighty mammalian species have disappeared. But these have disappeared due to dogs, goats, and rats, not man. As these animals, dogs, goats, and rats, have accompanied men to the new world, they have eliminated some animals. The dodo disappeared because of man, but it could have been rapidly killed off if some mongooses had reached Mauritius, or some predatory birds. It would have disappeared without man's help. Of flora, the poet William Blake said, "Where man is not, nature is barren." Men chronicle the destruction of forests by man, but not their creation by men. New York, known as a concrete jungle, has more than three million trees, no small number. Many lumber companies have replanted forests, and forests are commonly more healthy now than when North America was first settled.[5]

The Biblical faith is a vision and mandate of man as God's image bearer to exercise dominion over the earth (Gen. 1:26–28). This requirement has been warped by fallen man into a mandate to exercise dominion over other men. In the realm

---

5. Cy A. Adler, "Death by Falling Watermelons," in *Oui*, Vol. 5, No. 5, 1976, 55ff.

of mankind, the mandate is very different: "Wherefore putting away falsehood, speak ye truth each one with his neighbor: for we are members one of another" (Eph. 4:25). Bishop Westcott described Ephesians 4:4–6 as the Christian charter and law:

> There is one Body and one Spirit, even as ye were called in one hope of your calling: one Lord, one faith, one Baptism: one God and Father of all, who is over all, and through all and in all.

Westcott then declared:

> The fundamental image of "the body" guards us from many errors. The rich energy of the whole depends on the variety of the parts. There can be no physical or intellectual or moral equality among men as the members of the Body of Christ. Each man has his own peculiar function. Each man is heir of one past and has some unique heritage to administer and to hallow. The opportunity which we seek for him is not the opportunity of doing anything, but of doing that one thing which answers to his individuality and his place. As he does this he enters on the enjoyment of the fullness of the greater life to which he has contributed. Regarded under this aspect—the aspect of Christian Faith—life is an opportunity for service. We are not our own. We were not only redeemed by Christ: we were bought by Him, and are His. The essence of all sin lies in selfishness, self-assertion. Brought to this test the great questions of temperance and purity can be dealt with effectively. The virtues are positive and not negative. They are not personal but social. Any indulgence which lessens our own efficiency, or brings injury on another, is sinful. St. Paul has laid down the principles: "If because of meat thy brother is grieved, thou walkest no longer in love. Destroy not with thy meat him for whom Christ died…Overthrow not for meat's sake the work of GOD." (Rom. xiv.15, 20). And again: "Know ye not that your bodies are members of Christ? Shall I then take away the members of Christ and make them members of a harlot?" (I Cor. vi.15)[6]

---

6. Westcott, *op. cit.*, 57-54. Address on "The Incarnation a Revelation of Human Duties."

The goal of the incarnation is a new humanity in Christ. According to Paul:

> 18. For through him we both have access by one Spirit unto the Father.
> 19. Now therefore ye are no more strangers and foreigners, but fellow citizens with the saints, and of the household of God;
> 20. And are built upon the foundation of the apostles and prophets, Jesus Christ himself being the chief corner stone;
> 21. In whom all the building fitly framed together groweth unto a holy temple in the Lord:
> 22. In whom ye also are builded together for an habitation of God through the Spirit. (Eph. 2:18–22)

The welfare state seeks a one-world order by means of legislation, taxation, and coercive restrictions on men. It seeks to create community by external forces, whereas the one Body purposed by God in Christ comes from redemption, i.e., the regeneration and the sanctification of men. It is curious that men are cynical of this supernatural goal and action and so hopeful in the humanistic hope which has brought so much evil and coercion into history. Jesus Christ, the Lord of history, before His crucifixion, declared the total victory to ensue from His victory over sin and death: "And I, if I be lifted up from the earth, will draw all men unto me" (John 12:32). All men shall be one Body in Him, and the goal of His new humanity and of His law are plainly stated: to the end that there be "no poor among you" (Deut. 15:4).

SIXTEEN

THE PROBLEM OF POVERTY, PART 2

About forty years ago, late one night I saw an automobile parked near our driveway. In it were a man and wife, three children, and some bundles of clothing. It was a cold night. The man, who claimed he was a migrant worker, said that he had assumed the mountain road was a short cut, and he was now without food or gasoline. I took him into the house, gave the famished family a late supper, and they were bedded down for the night in the living room. In the morning, after breakfast, I gave them money for gasoline and lunch, and they left. The man stopped at a service station, identified himself as my guest and doing some work for me, gained a spare tire for his car on that basis, and left; the tire, of course, was unpaid for.

Unusual? On the contrary, this is a mild incident. I know of incidents where such recipients of Christian charity have received very extensive help and yet have robbed their benefactor and host, refused to work at the smallest and easiest task, have been guilty of savage child-beating, wife-beating, and more. Welfare offices of the county pay no attention to moral delinquency, criminal misconduct towards the family, or theft. As soon as various technical requirements are met and the papers are processed, such people receive housing and support. The men know that they are not going to be required to work; they refuse jobs and demand welfare as their "right."

It is very naïve to assume that such problems did not exist in the Roman Empire in New Testament times. They did, to a far-reaching degree. As a consequence of this, Paul wrote bluntly to the Thessalonian church:

> 10. For even when we were with you, this we commanded you, that if any would not work, neither should he eat.
> 11. For we hear that there are some which walk among you disorderly, working not at all, but are busybodies.
> 12. Now them that are such we command and exhort by our Lord Jesus Christ, that with quietness they work, and eat their own bread.
> 13. But ye, brethren, be not weary in well doing.
> (2 Thess. 3:10–13)

Some of the converts obviously expected to continue on welfare, and to exploit their Christian brethren as well. Such nonworkers were a problem to the community; they were "disorderly," and they were "busybodies." Paul's *command*, in the name of Christ the Lord, is that if able-bodied men would not work, they should not be fed. When Christians in the early church became jobless, the deacons provided them with money for one day's support, and, after that, work helping some Christian brother at below-standard pay. They were to be discouraged from dependency thereby.

From the earliest days of the church, widows (and orphans) who lacked a supporting family were cared for by "the daily ministrations" of the church. The deacons were named as the body of men in charge of this task (Acts 6:1–6). This help was not sentimental; it was not grounded in any *merit* in the poor, simply because *merit* was not the issue. At the same time, it did not condone evil, nor subsidize a refusal to work.

The premise of Christian charity must be the law of God and His requirement of us.

The case of Ruth is instructive. She performed the *duty* of a daughter to Naomi, although she was a daughter-in-law. In Ruth 2:1–23, we see that Boaz showed *respect* for Ruth's character, but he did not offer to support her nor Naomi: he simply favored her in the hard work of gleaning. There was respect for Ruth, and Ruth had the fact of work to indicate her own ability to care for herself and Naomi. Gleaning was harder work than harvesting, since harvesting means working with all the grain or fruit, whereas gleaning requires picking the remnant of the crop.

The poor in terms of whom God's law is given are those who are victims of disasters, deaths, and a variety of factors beyond their control. Some, who cannot work, need constant help, whereas others are to be helped in order to gain work, or helped to work. Such poor people often gain *less* help than others simply because they are not demanding help as "a right." The *U. S. News and World Report,* January 11, 1988, reported on about nine million such people, mostly white and *working,* predominantly devout Christians, and of good character. Such people trouble the consciences of many, whereas those who will not work and insist on welfare as their right are "no problem," because the state, after a fashion, cares for them. Proverbs tells us,

> The poor is hated even of his own neighbour: but the rich hath many friends. (Prov. 14:20)

> All the brethren of the poor do hate him: how much more do his friends go far from him? he pursueth them with words, yet they are wanting to him. (Prov. 19:7)

Very few appreciate the extent to which individual Christians as well as churches and other Christian ministries seek to help the poor and needy. Statistics on the financial amount of the help are very faulty: they only report on what official Christian agencies do, not on the work of individuals. Moreover, the work of *major* church bodies is the usual extent of such reports. Some of this work is highly competent, as witness the Salvation Army, or *ad hoc*, i.e., with respect to a specific need and crisis. Thus, in Stockton, California, every afternoon at about three o'clock, Veltessia Smith, a Christian woman (black), feeds about one hundred fifty or so hungry people in the downtown area. Prayer precedes the meal. This is the work of the Christ Temple Apostolic Faith Church. Police have regularly interfered, declaring that a license is necessary for such charitable work, whereas clerks at city hall as regularly state that no such law exists. Some objectors to the feeding claim that the downtown park is left in "one hell of a mess," although the men who eat there are required to clean up after themselves, and no signs of litter remain.

> Joe Jackson said he was there every day, and every day he helped clean up.
>
> "We know the cops are watching us," he said. "There's a lot of hungry people down here. We ain't going to let it stop because of that," he said.
>
> Sharif Muhammad also eats at the park. He is among the thankful.
>
> "Believe me, I've been hungry," he said. "Now, at least I can go to sleep without the hunger on my mind. It gets bad. Bad enough to make you go out and take someone else's possessions. Hunger makes you angry and short-fused and mean.
>
> "The harmony I feel here is about family. I just can't believe anybody is against this," he said.
>
> Elizabeth Wilder said, "There's a lot of starving people around here. They can't make her stop. They can't."[1]

---

1. Keith Robson, "Food crew gets mixed blessings," in *The Stockton* (California) *Record,* Saturday, January 23, 1988, A-1, A-4.

Given the Christian and personal context of this giving, it is not surprising that some of the poor are grateful. People who have worked in state welfare offices have reported that the most depressing aspect of their work is the routine ingratitude. Not a few of the welfare workers enter the field full of zeal, eager to help the needy. Too many become hard and cynical after a time, or leave for other lines of work because of their disillusionment.

We have two kinds of poor today, as did Rome, for example. Rome's economic and military policies destroyed its strength, i.e., its small, independent farmers. From a people with many hard-working landowners and workers, they became a nation with extremes of wealth and poverty. The hard-working small farmers became the city poor, the welfare mobs and circus and arena fans. From an asset they became a liability and a threat to the security of Rome. Later emperors located their working capitol outside of Rome.

In the modern era, we again have two kinds of poor, *first*, the welfare people, and, *second*, the working poor reported on by *U. S. News and World Report.* These working poor increasingly include many blacks as the black churches continue their work of converting many of the inner city blacks from welfarism to work. This represents a major fact on the American scene. Churches, commonly small and intensely devout evangelical groups, are increasingly ministering to the welfare poor and converting them. In city slum areas, some of these converts are doing remarkable things. Older women, unable often to work and continuing on state welfare, have successfully cleaned up their streets and apartment buildings of narcotic dealers, prostitutes, hoodlums, and youth gangs. They have organized groups to remove trash and improve the buildings. Their efforts are notable and courageous. At the same time, other converts who are able to work have left welfare, at times for lesser incomes, in order to effect their family's rehabilitation.

The Stockton, California, church mentioned earlier, the Christ Temple Apostolic Faith Church, is one of a great number of like small churches from coast to coast who are saving the lost, caring for the needy, and feeding the hungry. Sociologists and historians show no appreciation for, nor awareness of, what these often unacknowledged churches are doing, and they are therefore ignorant of what is happening. Very simply, these churches are doing the Lord's work. The poor are helping the poor.

SEVENTEEN

Compassion

The word *compassion* has suffered from liberal misuse in the post-World War II era. The word is common to the Bible and translates several Hebrew and Greek words, and it deserves rehabilitation. Liberals use the word to justify legislation, whereas in its Biblical origins its meaning relates to personal attitudes and action. Some of the words used in the Bible are

1. *chamal* (khawmal), to commiserate, have compassion, pity; to spare. Hebrew.

2. *racham* (rawkham), from the root to fondle, to love compassionately, to be merciful, to have pity. Hebrew.

3. *racham* (rakham), from no. 2, with the same implications but implying the womb and the unborn babe, tender love and caring. Hebrew.

4. *rachuwm* (rakhoom), from no. 2., *full* of compassion and mercy. Hebrew.

5. *splagchnizomai,* Greek, to have bowels, or yearn, feel sympathy and pity, to be moved.

6. *eleeo* (eleheho), Greek, to have compassion, pity, or mercy

7. *oikteiro,* Greek, to exercise compassion, pity.

8. *metriopatheo,* Greek, to be gentle and treat kindly, to be compassionate.

9. *sumpatheo,* Greek, having a fellow feeling, to have compassion.

10. *sumpathes,* Greek, mutually commiserate and compassionate.

In the context of their use, these words refer to more than feeling; they are a part of the requirement of community under the triune God and His law.

Now the word *compassion* is a key to the history of Christianity and hence very important. The requirement for compassion came from God's law, but Christianity gave it a new and working focus. In the synagogue, the leader assigned visitors to members for hospitality, but in the church the "bishop" had to be "a lover of hospitality" (Titus 1:7–8). Members of the order of widows had to have a history of caring for the strangers and the afflicted (1 Tim. 5:10). The apostles took works of compassion so seriously that it interfered with their ministerial work, and the order of deacons was established (Acts 6:1–6).

This emphasis on compassion did not impress the Greco-Roman elite. For them, it marked all Christians as lower class, despite the presence of many very superior men among them. Paul's status as a Christian, for example, was a matter of amazement to some Romans.

While the vast population of slaves and poor people responded at times with startled attention and approval to the compassion of Christians, the leaders were repelled by it. As Goodenough noted, "The elite structure could not live side-by-side with Christian compassion."[1] Two motives were thus in conflict, Roman elitism versus Christian compassion.

These two forces are with us still, but in altered forms. Elitism in Rome dealt with the poor with political motives: it provided bread and circuses to keep the poor satisfied and safe. Elitism in the modern world is as contemptuous of the poor as any noble Roman, but it shows the effects of Christian civilization. *Compassion* is now a socially approved and politically necessary virtue, and its expression is statist welfarism. The goal is to satisfy the poor, and to keep them far from the rich. Compassion has thus become an instrument of elitism rather than of Christian community.

Two alien faiths and hopes lie behind elitism and Christianity. The elitist wants to alleviate need and maintain political and social order. His hope is that education and social action will in time elevate the poor masses to a higher and more rational level. Golby and Purdue have pointed out that in England, while Christian reforms worked to make men *more godly* and thereby to raise them out of their poverty and sin, the Enlightenment men placed their hope in making men *more rational*.[2] The goal thus became financial security for the family so that respectability would follow, a goal some Christians also gave assent to.[3] A variety of institutions were created to further this goal.[4] As against state welfarism and education, Christians who were pioneers in both charity and education placed their essential hope on regeneration. A good society requires regenerate men, a godly people. Thus, two alien faiths were in conflict. Kingsley saw the difference:

> It is much cheaper and pleasanter to be reformed by the devil than by God; for God will only reform society on the condition of our reforming every man his own self—while

---

1. Simon Goodenough, with Richard Reece, *Citizens of Rome* (New York, NY: Crown Publishers, 1979), 10.
2. J. M. Golby and A. W. Purdue, *The Civilization of the Crowd, Popular Culture in England 1750-1900* (London, England: Batsford, 1984), 10.
3. Ibid., 178.
4. Ibid., 178—19, 196ff.

> the devil is quite ready to help us mend the laws and the parliament, earth and heaven, without ever starting such an impertinent and "personal" request, as that a man should mend himself.[5]

In the elitist tradition, various alternatives have been used to reform society by means of the state: education, welfarism, legislation, and revolution. Christian socialism very early tried to unite Biblical faith with Enlightenment humanism. In time, of course, the Christian emphasis was shelved.

> The suggestion "for the peaceful regeneration of the race by the cultivation of individual character"—I am quoting from Bernard Shaw's history of the Fabian Society—was not accepted. "Certain members of that circle," says Shaw, "modestly feeling that the revolution would have to wait an unreasonably long time if it postponed until they personally had attained perfection, set up the banner of Socialism militant."[6]

Compassion thus ceased to be a Christian concern for many; it ceased to be essentially a personal religious concern, however expressed in person, by the church, or by some Christian agency, and it became a political and economic cause. The agency of compassion became the state.

In this process, however, something was lost. The word *compassion* continues in use, but its root meaning, to bear, to suffer with, by personal action has given way to legislative action which distances the poor, the sick, and the needy from us. But this is not all. The statist emphasis has meant the priority of politico-economic determination. As a result, morality, the foundation of Christian compassion, now is seen as economically determined. Thus Harrison, in discussing marriage, agrees with Marx that the ideas of the ruling class are the governing ideas, and these are materialistically or economically determined. Thus, sexual codes and marriage, like

---

5. Charles Kingsley, "Parson Lot," *Letters to Chartists*, no. 1, 1848; cited in Karl de Schweinitz, *England's Road to Social Security*, (New York, NY: A. S. Barnes, 1943), 140.

6. Ibid., 174.

all morality, are created to protect the ruling class and their interests.[7]

We live in an era when remarkable instances of compassion can be found all over the world. An occasional Christian, such as Mother Teresa, not at all unusual in her accomplishments, gains public attention, but most, Catholic and Protestant, are neglected or harassed; the extent of their importance is belittled quite commonly. A Mother Teresa is not presented as an instance of centuries old and commonplace Christian grace in action but as a romantic tale. Such an approach actually belittles the nature and scope of Christian compassion.

The modern attitude has deep roots. An incident reflecting the envy and resentment for the power of Charles Borromeo by the representative of King Philip of Spain, the Marquis de Ayamonte, is telling:

> Charles Borromeo's life, too, was an example of sudden and dramatic changes of fortune. It might have been expected that after the plague, when he had become the idol of the people, the rest of his life would have slipped away in peace and popularity. Ayamonte had come back to Milan, had helped to carry the canopy over the Archbishop in the Holy Nail procession of May, 1577, had received from him a facsimile of the Nail as a sign of renewed friendship (October, 1577). Yet, when the city was at last free from the plague, he said to the Archbishop, with an all but incredible mixture of rudeness and stupidity, "It is most painful for me to see how everyone in Milan loves you. You are most worshipped, while I, I, the minister of the most powerful king, am barely tolerated..."
>
> As early as March that year, Borromeo had been told that Ayamonte had so poisoned Philip's mind that he talked of asking the Pope to remove this ambitious priest from Milan. "That is no news to me," had been Borromeo's answer.[8]

---

7. Fraser Harrison, *Dark Angel, Aspects of Victorian Sexuality* (London, England: Sheldon Press, 1977), 272.

8. Margaret Yeo, *Reformer, St. Charles Borromeo* (Milwaukee, WS: The Bruce Publishing Company, 1938), 33–34.

Besides his work during the plague, when 17,000 died in Milan, 8,000 in the neighboring countryside, and 120 priests, Borromeo's charities included the following: a hostel for beggars and tramps, orphanages for boys and for girls, a home for reformed prostitutes, another for homeless girls, and, interestingly enough, a home for unhappily married women. He also provided dowries to enable penniless girls to marry; otherwise, they would have been pushed into prostitution. He originated the idea of a state pawnshop for the poor to help them escape usurious pawnbrokers.[9] Borromeo was a man of his time; his view of Protestants, with whom he had little contact, was conventional. He regarded the Turks as less dangerous than Luther and Calvin![10] All the same, when confronted by human need and suffering, like many equally narrow Protestants of his day, he was a man of compassion.

Statist "compassion," if it could be called that, led to serious and abiding problems which helped destroy Rome. The same elitist compassion is basic to many problems of state today. The Christians did not waste time warring against Roman welfarism. They were men of compassion and charity, and they stressed the regeneration of men and nations by Jesus Christ.

9. Ibid., 228–29.
10. Ibid., 174.

EIGHTEEN

SOLUTIONS

To believe that man-made problems can be solved is a sound and legitimate belief in most cases. Of course, we cannot reverse time and events to undo the evil done, but many problems are capable of a solution. There are, however, problems in solving problems. *First,* too many people want instant answers and solutions. Our Lord tells us, "For the earth bringeth forth fruit of herself; first the blade, then the ear, after that the full corn in the ear" (Mark 4:28). We cannot reap a harvest immediately after the seed is sown. Growth takes time, and so does problem solving. Quick and superficial "solutions" can lead to more serious problems.

Second, solutions are sometimes more desired than resolutions, i.e., a desire to make peace can lead to a forced harmony. In too many instances, a guilty person is allowed to make an apology without restitution, or reconciliation is insisted on without even a trace of regret on the part of the guilty party.

Many other false forms of solutions can be cited, but our central concern is, *third,* that solutions which evade the central moral issue are both false and evil. Education in our day is humanistic; therefore, at its best it is technical and factual, not Christian. The modern era began with an exaltation of mathematics, a legitimate area of study but hardly a discipline to condition all others. In school we are taught that two plus two equals four, which is true enough, but very few answers in life are as easy or as abstract. In high school geometry, I heard some students express a desire that all life and thought could be reduced, like geometry, to a handful of axioms and propositions. Over the generations, men like Spinoza have tried to do just that. But two plus two equals four is an abstraction and a technical answer. Most of man's problems are neither technical nor abstractions; they are moral and personal.

What answers are possible when man is resolutely evil? How can a family crisis be resolved when the members are all evil and persistent in their evil? What answer is there to rulers who are evil and have most people on their side? Again, when churchmen are evil, how can the church be other than evil? Very often, reform and change are the least desired solutions! To expect answers then is itself evil. It is rather a time for judgment *and* rebuilding.

The Wall Street Journal, February 3, 1988, carried a long report on the abuse of elderly people, often by their children. One woman had a two-inch scar on her forehead; she had been struck by an iron skillet. A jagged mark on the nose and under one eye came from a kick with a steel-towed shoe. This injury put her into a hospital for a month. The guilty parties were her son and daughter-in-law. The woman was not allowed to use her own stove or refrigerator and ate at a neighbor's. On occasion, she had been locked out of her own apartment. The woman, however, refuses to file charges against her son, so that his evil is matched by her evil in condoning the offense.

A congressional subcommittee estimates the number of such assaults to be about one million one hundred thousand a year, with the reported cases of such "abuse" increasing rapidly. Some cases result in death.[1]

---

1. Clare Ausberry, "Family Affair, Abuse of the Elderly by Their Own Chiidren Increases in America," *The Wall Street Journal*, Wednesday, February 3, 1988, Western edition, 1, 12.

Legislation will not remove such problems from a civilization. *First,* while laws punishing such offenses exist and are necessary, the laws are solving nothing. Even when the injured file charges, no real change occurs all too often. Probation or a short sentence may follow, and then the consequences are worse. The angry criminal exacts his revenge too often. Court orders forbidding any molestation or return to the house are routinely ignored.

Second, the basic problem of *evil* is not resolved. The problem of sin is not solvable on a technical basis. It is not a two plus two problem. It requires the regeneration of a man to be resolved. It is true that some who are poor and needy respond with gratitude when they are helped. It is also true that some respond with evil, with a desire to hurt and exploit their Good Samaritan as a fool. "Don't expect me to be grateful," one woman contemptuously told a woman who helped, and wanted to see the woman use the help constructively. A man, after exploiting and robbing his benefactor said, "We both got something out of this; you got the satisfaction of doing good, and I got the satisfaction I wanted."

Does this mean that we should cease from doing good, or from being charitable? By no means, but it requires us to recognize that sin exists on all sides and in all kinds of men. Being in a pitiable condition makes no man good. If we assume that our charity or goodness will change people, then we are, like statist welfare workers, thinking humanistically. No man's goodness can change the heart of another man. Only God can.

If we place the primary emphasis of our charity on charity itself, i.e., the *fact* of help to others, we go astray. Similarly, we cannot make pity our primary motivation. Divorced from a theological context, pity readily becomes sentimentality and has, as William Blake wanted, merely a human face. It is humanism in action, and, in that form, pity for the needy can easily combine with hatred for the affluent.

In the Bible, compassion or pity is always associated with grace. Having received the grace of God, we manifest it to others. We too often hear of people who show compassion to the poor and needy, but less often that their motivation is grace. When grace is our motivation, we know the limitations of our efforts, and how limited is the good we can do, and how great God's power and works. As we survey the evil in men both high and low, we know that the resolution lies in God's sovereign grace. For us then, the necessity is to recognize that the cross means judgment on sin. If God the Son, as man's last Adam, undergoes judgment for His people, how can men and nations expect to evade judgment for sin? We know they shall be judged. Our duty is to obey our Lord, be charitable where we can, and to know that, however miserable may be the results that we see, in Jesus Christ, our "labour is not in vain" but will accomplish His purpose (1 Cor. 15:58). Our work is thus one of reconstruction, knowing that the design is not of us but the Lord.

NINETEEN

Widows, Orphans, and the Poor

Like the pagan Romans who saw the present and the future commanded by Christians, contemporary humanistic scholars, sensing the threat to their statist world order, lash out savagely against Christianity. R. L. Rike, in *Apex Omnium: Religion in the Res Gestae of Ammianus*, studies the history written by the pagan Roman, Ammianus Marcellinus, at the end of the fourth century A.D. In a long review article, J. W. Jamieson agrees with Ammianus and Edward Gibbon, in *The Decline and Fall of the Roman Empire*, in blaming the fall of Rome on Christianity. Rike presents Ammianus' thesis with apparent favor. Roman paganism was an ethnic religion, a religion of the family and the state; like Shintoism, it was a racial or ethnic faith, limited to one people, and hence it was not missionary minded nor other than aristocratic. Christianity, however, was (and is) missionary minded, and, according to Rike and Jamieson, equalitarian as against the racial inequalitarianism of ethnic religions. Loyalty to Jesus Christ replaced loyalty to the Roman state and its emperor. Ammianus saw ethnic faiths as superior. "By contrast, Christianity is a worthless religion which serves not to strengthen but to weaken the empire."[1] Rike, according to Jamieson, sees with Ammianus Christianity as "a distraction from the task of *imperium.*"[2]

Modern paganism is still extensively colored by Biblical premises, consciously or unconsciously. Our modern humanistic statism, whether Marxist or democratic, professes to rule in the name of the people. Curiously, the people have less and less place in the plans of these new elitists. Like Roman welfarism of old, modern welfare does not bond the recipients to the donors. Statist welfarism establishes no personal relationship. It is this personal relationship as "members one of another" (Eph. 4:25) that Christianity fosters, not equalitarianism as such. This is clearly apparent in James 2:1–10:

> 1. My brethren, have not the faith of our Lord Jesus Christ, the Lord of glory, with respect of persons.
> 2. For if there come unto our assembly a man with a gold ring, in goodly apparel, and there come in also a poor man in vile raiment;
> 3. And ye have respect to him that weareth the gay clothing, and say unto him, Sit thou here in a good place; and say to the poor, Stand thou there, or sit here under my footstool:
> 4. Are ye not then partial in yourselves, and are become judges of evil thoughts?
> 5. Hearken, my beloved brethren, Hath not God chosen the poor of this world rich in faith, and heirs of the kingdom which he hath promised to them that love him?
> 6. But ye have despised the poor. Do not rich men oppress you, and draw you before the judgment seats?
> 7. Do not they blaspheme that worthy name by the which ye are called?
> 8. If ye fulfil the royal law according to the scripture, Thou shalt love thy neighbour as thy self, ye do well:
> 9. But if ye have respect to persons, ye commit sin, and are convinced of the law as transgressors.

---

1. J. W. Jamieson, "Early Christianity as Missionary Religion, Book Review Article," in *The Mankind Quarterly*, Vol. 28, no. 4, Summer, 1988, 418.
2. Ibid., 420.

> 10. For whosoever shall keep the whole law, and yet offend in one point, he is guilty of all.

Respect or regard of persons is repeatedly condemned in the law as a perversion of justice by judges (Deut. 1:17). This law also applies to human relations. To favor a person because of his wealth is to be "partial" and to "become judges of evil thoughts" (v. 4). In a fallen world, wealth is power, and such power is routinely used against believers (vv. 5–7). For Christians to show respect of persons is to acquiesce in the very evil which oppresses them. James is not asking for equalitarianism but for no respect of persons. There is a difference. That one man is a wealthy industrialist, and another is a very poor day laborer, is a fact which only communism can equalize, only to create greater evils. The Biblical concern is that both men must be seen from the Lord's perspective as alike in need of grace from Him, and of justice and mercy from us. To keep the royal law, to love our neighbor as ourselves (v. 8), means to respect his person, his family (Thou shalt not commit adultery), his property (Thou shalt not steal), his life (Thou shalt not kill), and his reputation (Thou shalt not bear false witness). It means also that, as members one of another, we are mindful of the needs of others.

There is a very important insight into this in Daniel. Daniel was asked by Nebuchadnezzar to interpret a strange dream, which he does, reluctantly. God, he tells the king, is bringing judgment upon him for two reasons:

> Wherefore, O king, let my counsel be acceptable unto thee, and break off thy sins by righteousness, and thine iniquities by shewing mercy to the poor; if it may be a lengthening of thy tranquillity. (Dan. 4:27)

First, Nebuchadnezzar lacks "righteousness" or justice. *Second,* he does not show "mercy to the poor." For these two reasons, God was destroying Nebuchadnezzar's mind for a time, until "understanding" in the form of justice, and "mercy to the poor," commanded his life and thought. Clearly, God regards these two things important enough to overthrow a Nebuchadnezzar for a season, and to bring down Rome.

It is interesting to note that in the medieval era charity was often imposed as a penance for sin on proud and arrogant lords. A delightful episode of such a penance occurred in the first half of the fourteenth century. Sir Eustace d'Ambreticourt stole a nun, Elizabeth of Juliers, a niece of Queen Philippa of England (wife of Edward III), and widow of John, Earl of Kent, out of her convent. He found a "hedge-priest," John Ireland, and he married them. As penance, Archbishop Islip required Elizabeth to recite daily the seven penitential psalms, the fifteen gradual psalms, the Litany, *Placebo* and *Dirge.*

> Archbishop Islip also required both of them to give freely to the poor whenever they had carnal intercourse. Word quickly spread of the benefits attendant upon their matrimonial exertions, and most mornings Eustace found himself cheered on by clamorous villagers.[3]

While Archbishop Islip's requirement involved some humor, his course of action had deep roots in church history.

Biblical faith requires repentance for sins, godly repentance being an inner sorrow joined to outward acts such as restitution and penance. Restitution requires a restoration with penalty of whatever has been stolen or destroyed. Where restitution could not be made because of the nature of the sin, penance became commonplace. Penance meant an outward profession of sorrow. While penance later became formal and less vital, in the early church it commonly had to be shown by charity to the poor. As Bingham noted,

> And because mercy and liberality to the poor was a great argument and evidence of repentance, this was always in eminent degree exacted of them (of penitents). Cyprian puts this among the other indications of repentance. "Can we think," says he, "that that man laments with his whole heart, and deprecates the Lord with fasting, weeping, and

---

3. Michael Packe, ed. by L. C. B. Seaman, *King Edward III*, (London, England: Routledge & Kegal Paul, 1983), 255.

> mourning, who, from the moment of his sinning, daily frequents the baths, who feeds himself with luxurious feasting, and fills his belly to an extraordinary pitch, only to belch forth his crudities the day after; who imparts not his meat and drink to the necessities of the poor? How does he bewail his own death, who walks about with a merry and cheerful countenance; who trims his beard and attires his face? Does he think to please men, who displeases God? Does that woman lament and mourn, who is at leisure to put on her costly clothing, and never thinks of the garment of Christ, which she has lost?" In such a case he thinks charity to the poor would be a more becoming ornament, than all their silks and jewels and gold; therefore he advises them to put on the ornament of Christ, that they might not appear naked before him.[4]

Cyprian stressed charity in writing to the clergy, saying,

> I request that you will diligently take care of the widows, and of the sick, and of all the poor. Moreover, you may supply the expenses for strangers, if any should be indigent, from my own portion, which I have left with Rogatianus, our fellow-presbyter...[5]

In his *Three Books of Testimonies Against the Jews,* Cyprian strongly stressed charity and tied it to being members one of another. Heading 3 is titled "That charity and brotherly affection are to be religiously and steadfastly practiced." Heading 113 reads:

> That the widow and orphan ought to be protected.
>
> In Solomon: "Be merciful to the orphan as a father, and as a husband to their mother; and thou shalt be the son of the Highest if thou shalt obey." (Ecclus. iv. 10) Also in Exodus: "Ye shall not afflict any widow or orphan. But if ye afflict them, and they cry out and call unto me, I will hear their

4. Joseph Bingham, *The Antiquities of the Christian Church,* Vol. 2, Book 18, Chapter 2, Sect. 10 (London, England: Reeves & Turner, 1878), 1064.

5. *The Ante-Nicene Fathers,* Vol. 5, *Hippolytus, Cyprian, Caius, Novatian,* Epistle 35 (Grand Rapids, MI: Eerdmans, 1981 reprint), 314.

> cryings, and will be angry in mind against you; and I will destroy you with the sword, and your wives shall be widows, and your children orphans." (Ex. xxii. 22-24) Also in Isaiah: "Judge for the fatherless, and justify the widow; and come, let us reason, saith the Lord." (Isa. i. 17–18) Also in Job: "I have preserved the poor man from the hand of the mighty, and I have helped the fatherless, who had no helper: the mouth of the widow hath blessed me." (Job xxix. 12–13) Also in the sixty-eighth Psalm: "The Father of the orphans, and the Judge of the widows." (Ps. lxviii. 5)[6]

Note Cyprian's reference to Exodus 22:22–24; v. 21 in that chapter requires justice for aliens. The penalty promised by God is the other side of the Golden Rule. In Obadiah 15, we read:

> For the day of the LORD is near upon all the heathen: as thou hast done, it shall be done unto thee: thy reward shall return upon thine own head.

This is related also to the judgment of Nebuchadnezzar. God declares in Exodus 22:21–24 that if men and societies oppress the poor, if they afflict the widow and the orphan, He will recompense them with death, and will make widows of their wives, and orphans of their children.

Quite obviously, this is not an insignificant matter to God. Rome did not fall because of the Christians, but by God's judgment and decree. Churchmen and nations had better take note.

---

6. *Ante-Nicene Christian Library,* Vol. 13, *The Writings of Cyprian,* Vol. 2, "Testimonies Against the Jews" (Edinburgh, Scotland: T. & T. Clark, 1873), 196. Cyprian's last citation is Psalm 68 in our numbering.

TWENTY

Charity, Part 1

Twentieth century man has had a very different view of himself than his forebears have had. *First* of all, especially since the Renaissance and Enlightenment, many among Western men saw themselves in terms of Greco-Roman humanism. In Shakespeare's *Hamlet,* we see Hamlet say concerning man,

> What a piece of work is man! How noble in reason! how infinite in faculties! in form and moving, how express and admirable in action, how like an angel! in apprehension, how like a god! the beauty of the world! the paragon of animals! And yet, to me, what is this quintessence of dust? man delights not me; nor woman neither. (Act II, scene II)

This statement represents Hamlet's bitterness that man falls so far short of what he is said to be; it reflects a late Renaissance perspective. A contemporary of Shakespeare, George Chapman, wrote a play entitled *Bussy D. Ambois,* about a Frenchman of a noble family. A flamboyant character who when quite young murdered a Huguenot cousin during the St. Bartholomew's Massacre, Bussy offended many important people and was in time himself murdered. Chapman may have had private sources of information in writing his play. In the play, the dying Bussy is dismayed that he is not immortal and declares that he will complain to God about it:

> Is my body, then,
> But penetrable flesh? And must my mind
> Follow my blood? Can my divine part add
> No aid to th' earthly in extremity?
> Then these divines are but for form, not fact.
> Man is of two sweet courtly friends compact,
> A mistress and a servant; let my death
> Define life nothing but a courtier's breath.
> Nothing is made of nought, of all things made,
> Their abstract being a dream but of a shade.
> I'll not complain to earth yet, but to Heaven,
> And, like a man, look upwards even in death.
> (Act V, scene IV)

Such thinking reflected the views of the Renaissance neoplatonists. Although set back somewhat by the Reformation, this view returned with the Enlightenment, although now it was Reason which represented the divine in the humanistic view of man. With modifications, this view persisted through the nineteenth century.

The *second* view of man which has been and is influential in Western civilization has been the Biblical doctrine of man as created in the image of God, a fallen and depraved being since Adam, and redeemable only by the atoning work and regenerating grace of God through Jesus Christ. Because of Adam's sin, all mankind fell into the estate of sin, misery, and death. In Christ they are restored and enabled to bring all things under the dominion of Christ the King. In the words of the Westminster Shorter Catechism, A 26, "Christ executeth the office of a king, in subduing us to himself, in ruling and defending us, and in restraining and conquering all his and our enemies."

The view of Renaissance and Enlightenment humanism has given way to that of modern humanism, a suicidal view.

Although prior to Freud, many thinkers spoke of man's *subconscious* mind, Freud rejected this concept in favor of the unconscious, which is not so much a repository of the conscious mind but a basic and primordial, primitive element in man. Man, instead of having a relationship through his mind with some kind of divine power was now seen as essentially related through his unconscious with ancient and subhuman motives, urges, and drives. The mind or reason of man, instead of being godlike, was seen as governed by primitive motives and racial instincts.

At the same time, the depreciation of man's personality which had begun in Karl Marx was furthered by John Dewey. For Marx, man was not the creation of God but of economic forces and could be regenerated only by the economic reorganization of society. This was a radical devaluation of man, who, from being the maker of society, became its product. From being a sinner, man was now one sinned against. John Dewey insisted on the prior value and importance of society as organized into a state over the individual. The intrusion of the individual into the problems of society was for Dewey usually invalid. Thus, he said and spoke of his assertion as a truism, "We all know how demoralizing charity is."[1] Dewey made this statement by contrasting being employed versus receiving charity, *not* by contrasting charity to welfarism. Only so could he view his statement as obviously true. Then, because of his false contrast, Dewey could insist on the state control of production and distribution, of wages and conditions of living, and more. He insisted on a guaranteed right to work, a minimum wage, and the control by the worker of his industry. "These three things, then, seem to me the essential minimum elements of an intelligent plan of social reorganization."[2] He called for, not a *planned* society, but a "*continuously planning* society."[3] He spoke of "the cult of individual success by means

---

1. John Dewey, *Intelligence in the Modern World* (New York, NY: The Modern Library, 1939), 417.
2. Ibid., 422.
3. Ibid., 431.

of individual effort" as against the reality of social planning.[4] The social nature of the individual was basic for Dewey. God did not create man, and man for Dewey did not create society; man was a creature of society, as was religion.

If what society organized into a state does is of essential value, and what man does as an individual is not, then it follows that welfarism is very important and personal and religious charities are either unimportant or bad. At the very least, there is a moral devaluation of what the person does.

John Kekes, a professor of Philosophy and Public Policy at the State University of New York, Albany, New York, wrote in 1987 on "Benevolence: A Minor Virtue." Kekes did not enter into a discussion of the state versus the person. Instead, he simply discussed benevolence as a moral act. He said of morality, "Morality requires us to act for the good of others." This definition makes clear his humanism. For a Christian, morality is to do the will of God as set forth in His law-word. As a result, for Kekes the question is, "Who are the others for whose good we are obligated to act?" As against the Christian and utilitarian views that benevolence must be extended "to all human beings and that the best hope of doing so lies in fostering benevolence in moral agents," Kekes says,

> My purpose here is to argue that this view is mistaken. Benevolence is not a particularly important virtue, and fostering it to the extent that many, but by no means all, Christians and utilitarians find desirable is fueled by sentimentalism and risks immorality. There is no good reason why we, as moral agents, should be benevolent toward the vast majority of mankind. To insist that nevertheless we should be benevolent is sentimental...[5]

To an extent, Christians can agree with this. But why is benevolence a minor virtue?

---

4. Ibid., 486; from Dewey's *Education and the Social Order*, a pamphlet published by the League for Industrial Democracy.

5. John Kekes, "Benevolence: A Minor Virtue," *Social Philosophy and Policy*, Vol. 4, No. 2, Spring, 1987, 21.

Kekes follows Enlightenment thinkers in viewing benevolence "as a basic human disposition." It is "a natural virtue, a basic, a given element of human nature," one which in most men overbalances the selfish traits.[6] Clearly, Kekes does not see man as fallen!

For Kekes, neither limited nor generalized benevolence are "particularly important means to the good of others." There are several other motives which lead us to seek the good of others: "a sense of duty, justice, decency, personal ideals, prudence, the desire to avoid guilt or shame are some others. Hence, although benevolence is a virtue, it is only a minor one."[7] Kekes nowhere tells us what is a major virtue, or whether a major virtue exists.

Whatever Kekes' personal beliefs, his framework is not surprising; it is a modern, non-theistic perspective. If God is missing from a philosophy or a faith, the framework of thought will be either radically individualistic or anarchist, or it will be equally emphatically statist. For the statist form of humanism, all major virtues are statist, even as for philosophical autarky, all man's thinking is important and moral when it is rational.

Charity is devalued in terms of either outlook. In terms of our modern worldviews, charity is either a denial of the individual's autarky, or an interference with policies of state. Christian agencies are accordingly treated with hostility unless they become recipients of state funds and limit their status by stressing humanistic concerns rather than the Gospel as they function as minions of the state.

The question is one of priority: to whom is the question addressed, to whom the challenge, "And who is my neighbour?" (Luke 10:29). In the Bible, *mercy* is always personal; it begins with God, and it manifests itself through the people of God.

---

6. Ibid., 23.
7. Ibid., 36.

TWENTY-ONE

The Diaconate, Charity, and Welfarism

Humanistic motives have often governed commendable causes within the church. Man seeks to gain an advantage over God even with his virtues and obedience. This motivation infects every area of thought at some time and in some form. In Mariolatry, for example, a significant aspect of devotion is the belief that Mary, a creature, can exercise a governing influence with God. Protestants are ready to criticize Mariolatry, and underrate the Virgin Mary, while themselves falling prey to a comparable error. Motherhood has been exalted to a somewhat sacred level, and a "mother's heart" given undue emphasis. Some Protestant mothers are insistent that God *will* answer a mother's prayer for her son; this is more a belief in the power of nagging than an example of Biblical faith.

In considering therefore the nature of Christian charity, it is necessary to remind ourselves that erroneous motives have entered in. The modern term, *philanthropy,* represents an example of this; it means, literally, love of man, whereas Biblical charity means essentially manifesting God's grace because we have received His grace. As our Lord *commands* us, "Freely ye have received, freely give" (Matt. 10:8). Christian charity is indeed a godly work, but it is also essentially a manifestation of grace. We give because we have received.

When James tells us that faith without works is dead (James 2:14–16), he is declaring their virtual identity. A living faith reveals itself in a man's work: no faith, no works, and vice versa. The work of grace is a fruit of grace. A false separation leads to bad theology. Works separated from faith is philanthropy, and it is also a fallacious view of salvation at times. Faith separated from works tends to mysticism, or at least the confusion of experience and feeling with faith.

The early church was remarkable in its practice of charity. This was in part its inheritance from Judaism, but it went far beyond Judaism in the scope of its practice. We cannot underrate the importance of its work here. At the same time, this practice was not error free. For example, St. John Chrysostom declared:

> Are you unable to practise the virginal life? Then make a prudent marriage. Are you unable to do without possessions? Give, then of what you possess. Is such a burden too heavy for you? Divide your goods with Christ. Are you not willing to cede Him everything? Make over to Him at least the half or third part. He is your brother and co-heir; make Him your co-heir even on earth. How much soever you give to Him you give that to yourself.[1]

The neoplatonism and asceticism here is obvious. A life of marriage and the possession of property is the lesser way of spirituality, and amends can be made by living meagerly. God *requires* the tithes; gifts were possible only if more than a tithe were involved. Chrysostom urges "*at least* the half or third part" be given to Christ and His work. This is being holier than God!

With reference to true almsgiving, Chrysostom said:

> Charity is, indeed, a great thing, and a gift of God, and when it is rightly ordered, likens us to God Himself as far as that is possible; for it is charity which makes the man.

1. "Homilies on St. Matthew," from Mary H. Allies, translator, *Leaves from St. John Chrysostom* (London, England: Burns & Oates, 1889), 73.

> Some one, at least, wishing to characterise man, did it in these words: *Man is great, and the merciful man is honourable.* Kindness is better than raising up the dead. For it is a much greater thing to feed Christ in His hunger than to raise the dead in the name of Jesus. By feeding Christ you confer a benefit upon Him; in the other case He is benefiting you. And the reward is for doing, not receiving. As to the signs, you are under an obligation to God, but with regard to the almsgiving, you put God under an obligation to you.
>
> It is an alms when you give willingly, generously—thinking that you are rather taking than giving; when you give as if you were receiving something, as gaining rather than losing, otherwise there would be no thanks in it. He who helps his neighbour should be in gladness, not in gloom. In truth, is it not foolish that in removing the despondency of another you yourself should be despondent. You will not suffer it to be a real alms.[2]

In these words, a great impetus for subsequent charities is in evidence: "with regard to the almsgiving, *you put God under an obligation to you.*" This is a far cry from our Lord's words, "Freely ye have received, freely give."

This view of Chrysostom's is different from the emphasis of St. Ephrem of Syria, who said of Christ's birthday, "On this day to us came forth the Gift, although we asked it not! Let us therefore alms bestow on them that cry and beg of us."[3] Ephrem said also:

> He the Lord of all giveth all to us. He that enricheth all, requireth usury of all. He giveth to all things as wanting nothing, and yet requireth usury of all as if needy. He gave us herds and flocks as Creator, and yet asked sacrifices as though in need.[4]

This is closer in spirit to "Freely ye have received, freely give." Grace is stressed rather than putting God under an obligation.

---

2. "Homilies on St. Paul's Second Epistle to the Corinthians," in Ibid., 70.

3. "Rhythm the First," from J. B. Morris, translator, Select Works of *S. Ephrem the Syrian* (Oxford, England: John Henry Parker, 1847), 9.

4. Ibid., "Third Rhythm," 25.

Both views were widely prevalent, but, in time, the view of Chrysostom (not original with him, no doubt), prevailed. Centuries later, the Spanish picaresque writer, Mateo Aleman, wrote: "to the rich are given temporal goods and to the poor are given spiritual goods, so that in return for distributing earthly possessions among the poor, grace is bought."[5]

This does not mean that good did not flow out of this theological error, not necessarily because of the error but the faith still present with it. Maureen Flynn's study of Catholic confraternities in Zamora, Spain, 1400-1700, is a remarkable account of the Christian organization of life. The confraternities were mutual aid brotherhoods and sisterhoods; they included most Zamorans. Their work included mutual insurance, charitable activities, hospitals, burials, redeeming captives, maintaining bridges, providing dowries, preventing vengeance, and more. They owned land and properties to further their work. They had their own priests and were a lay-operated church outside the church. The French Revolution abolished all such organizations, among other corporations.[6]

Confraternities declined for a number of reasons. *First*, the plague made labor scarce, and this helped destroy the medieval attitude towards "holy poverty." *Second*, this went hand in hand with a changed attitude towards work, "and its value in the material development of nations."[7] Work was now more sanctifying, especially to Protestants, than was poverty, and able-bodied beggars were now regarded unfavorably.

There was also, *third*, the rise of statist charities, quickly becoming welfarism, as the state gained power, and as crisis conditions in the economy made the burden of charity too great for sometimes weakened church agencies.

Some legislation against begging followed in many countries. In Spain, a Dominican friar, Domingo de Soto, opposed such legislation on both theological and practical grounds.

---

5. Maureen Flynn, *Sacred Charity, Confraternities and Social Welfare in Spain 1400-1700* (Ithaca, NY: Cornell University Press, 1989), 76.

6. Ibid., 247.

7. Ibid., 86.

"He considered begging a fundamental human right of which no government should deprive its citizens."[8] Even more Soto saw begging as closely tied to property freedom. "As long as private property remained the foundation of the economic order, the poor could not be deprived of their private right to appeal for sustenance."[9]

At the same time also the Council of Trent began to alter the confraternities from lay control and lay concerns to ecclesiastical ones. In fact, in Flynn's telling words, "The universal brotherhood of brothers in Spain posed almost as great a threat to Catholic clergymen as the universal priesthood conceived by the Protestants," since the confraternities were administering sacraments and arranging their own services of worship.[10]

Calvin, meanwhile, was giving a renewed emphasis to charity. In his *Institutes*, Calvin declared, in terms of Acts, that

> The invariable custom, therefore, was, that no assembly of the Church should be held without the word being preached, prayers being offered, the Lord's supper administered, and alms given.[11]

Charity was thus made inseparable from worship. Very soon, Geneva saw the needy cared for. It was a cooperative task of church and state, as was the case in Spain. The work was under the jurisdiction of the church's diaconate. A paid, full-time deacon administered the charity.[12] Calvin believed that charity had to be an aspect of the life of faith and dependent on "the voluntary spirit."[13] He also held that work was essential, and, in a sermon on Deuteronomy 24:1–6, declared, "If a man is deprived of his work he is degraded."[14] Thus, efforts were made

---

8. Ibid., 95.

9. Ibid., 96.

10. Ibid., 118.

11. John Calvin, *Institutes of the Christian Religion*, Book 4, Chapter 17, Vol. 2 (Philadelphia, PA: Presbyterian Board of Christian Education, 1936), 705.

12. Ronald S. Wallace, *Calvin, Geneva, and the Reformation* (Edinburgh, Scotland: Scottish Academic Press, 1988), 90.

13. Ibid., 96.

14. Ibid., 124.

to provide work for the poor. Calvin's Geneva provided a pattern in Milan for Cardinal (later Saint) Charles Borromeo.

When the earlier, medieval, view of holy poverty gave way after the plague to a growing dislike of beggars, and a belief that able-bodied men should work, society was ready for a theology of work. Calvin laid the foundations for this in holding that poverty, instead of giving holiness to a man, degraded him.

Wallace said of Calvin that his program for Geneva could be described as one of social sanctification, and as having two aspects. The *first* was to be the personal transformation of the people. The *second* was to be through social discipline, "and through the sacramental power of the word of God."[15] The "social discipline" included the work of the diaconate.

Calvin's vision of society was one of church and state alike in the service of the triune God. Another concept was in the process of developing, however. In Flynn's terms, in describing its Spanish manifestation, in the new temper, "religion was conceived of as at the service of the state."[16] This meant social discipline for the peace of the state; not for peace with God. It led to a transition from godly charity to philanthropy and welfarism.

Humanistic advocates of welfarism would to a degree give their approval to Calvin's statement, but with a difference. *First*, for the humanistic statist, it is powerlessness *more* than worklessness which is degrading to a man. As a result, entitlements and aid replace work as the remedy for the poor. *Second*, Calvin saw man's degradation and prosperity in terms of man's status before God, not in terms of cash and material goods.

As a result, welfarism has degraded a man far more than poverty had, because its damage has been to the spirit of man.

---

15. Ibid., 31.
16. Flynn, *op. cit.*, 107.

TWENTY-TWO

CHARITY, PART 2

The Roman Empire, given its presuppositions, had good reasons for persecuting Christianity. It was an empire within the empire, with its own law code, the Bible, and its own king, Jesus Christ. Rome had serious problems: these were economic, among other things, plus the growing numbers of welfare recipients. Welfarism did not create loyalty to Rome. Rather, it created a growing mob of peoples whose life's purpose was to gain more from the empire.

As against this, another empire, Christianity, was providing health, education, and welfare. Christian charity created personal ties whereas welfarism dissolved them, and the result was social decay.

To be a member of a Christian church meant training as a catechumen to assume authority for the assistance of those in need. Stuart G. Hall has written,

> The candidates were examined individually to see "whether they lived piously while catechumens, whether they honoured the widows (that is, contributed to charity), whether they visited the sick, whether they fulfilled every

> good work"; if so they may "hear the gospel," apparently not previously allowed in this church, and must attend for daily exorcism (for this and what follows, see Hippolytus, Apostolic Tradition, 20-1). In other churches tests might be applied.[1]

To be a member, one had to be a *practicing* Christian. He was *taught* the faith but was excluded from communion and, apparently in Rome, from the preaching service unless he was active in charity. This account comes from a Roman theologian, Hippolytus, c. 200 A.D.

The *Didache*, which originates from the first to the mid-second century, required Christians to support their clergy in their ministry and charitable work. Lacking a prophet (or, preacher), they were to give directly to the poor:

> And every true prophet who wishes to settle among you deserves his food. 2. Similarly, a true teacher also deserves, like the laborer, his food (cf. Matt. 10:10b). 3. Take, therefore, every first fruit—of the produce of wine press and threshing floor and of cattle and sheep—and give it to the prophets. For they are your high priests. 4. But if you have no prophet, give to the poor. 5. If you make a batch of dough, take the "first fruit" and give it in accord with the commandment. 6. Similarly with a jug of wine or of oil, take the "first fruit" and give to the prophets. 7. And so with money, clothing, and every possession—take whatever "first fruit" seems appropriate to you and give it in accord with the commandment.[2]

With good reason, Hall could write, "In fact the local church was in many ways a charitable society."[3] He added,

> The vulnerable members of society, such as widows, orphans, surplus babies and elderly slaves, could be sure of a

1. Stuart G. Hall, *Doctrine and Practice in the Early Church* (Grand Rapids, MI: Eerdmans, [1991] 1992), 18.

2. Robert A. Kraft, *The Apostolic Fathers, A New Translation and Commentary*, Vol. 3, *Barnabas and the Didache* (New York: NY: Thomas Nelson & Sons, 1965), 172.

3. Hall, *op. cit.*, 23.

> livelihood if they belonged to the church. There the needy had a family which would see that they were not destitute.[4]

This enables us to understand why the emperor, Julian the Apostate, demanded that the pagan priests emulate the Christians: establish hospitals, care for the sick and strangers, and help the poor. Julian offered to help the pagan priests with money to do so, but the response was disheartening to him. The Emperor Constantine had earlier used his money to help both Christians and pagans; he gave food and clothing to the poor; took care of widows and orphans, and apparently provided dowries to the daughters of widows, according to Eusebius in his *Life of Constantine.*

Biblical law stressed works of charity, and this emphasis is strong in the New Testament. Early in the ministry of our Lord, John the Baptist sent two of his disciples to Jesus,

> 3. And said unto him, Art thou he that should come, or do we look for another?
> 4. Jesus answered and said unto them, Go and shew John again those things which ye do hear and see:
> 5. The blind receive their sight, and the lame walk, the lepers are cleansed, and the deaf hear, the dead are raised up, and the poor have the gospel preached to them.
> (Matt. 11:3–5)

Jesus gives evidence of His messiahship in two ways: *First,* miraculous attestations occur; healing comes to the lame, to lepers, to the blind, and to the deaf, and the dead are raised up. *Second,* the good news is preached to the poor. In the parable of judgment in Matthew 25:31–46, our Lord makes clear that inasmuch as we visit the imprisoned, clothe the naked, and give food and drink to the needy, we have done it unto Him. The ministry is more than preaching; it is faith in action. Whereas Greek thought was intellectual, whereas it stressed the mind, or *the head,* Christian faith stressed *the head and the hand,* faith and life, theology in action. "Thou shalt love thy neighbour as thyself" is not only in the Old Testament law, in

---

4. Idem.

Leviticus 19:18, but in the New Testament, in Matthew 5:43–44, and 19:19, in Luke 10:27, Mark 12:31, Romans 13:9, Galatians 5:14, and James 2:8.

There is much in the literature of the early church about exorcism which is too often read in modern terms, as having to do with demonic possession. While this was a facet of its meaning, we are too prone to ascribe undue connotations to the term. The candidate for church membership was anointed with the oil of exorcism and declared: "I renounce thee, Satan, and all thy servants, and all thy works."[5] Exorcism was the renunciation of one way of life for another, a life of law-keeping and brotherly love. A neglected meaning of exorcism is warding off evil powers, and the catechumen was taught, among other things, to ward off evil powers by godly faith and works, by charity. Much of medieval charity had this motivation.

The early church did not hold to salvation by charitable activities but rather affirmed that a true faith revealed itself in charity, whereas it was of no benefit to the ungodly:

> XLIII. These things we say concerning the pious; for as to the ungodly, if thou givest all the world to the poor, thou wilt not benefit him at all. For to whom the Deity was an enemy while he was alive, it is certain it will be so also when he is departed; for there is no unrighteousness with him. For "the Lord is righteous, and has loved righteousness."[6]

We cannot understand the continuing emphasis on charity during the Christian centuries apart from the strong faith and works, head and hand, emphasis. Patristic literature abounds with such teachings, e.g.,

> XII. If thou hast by the work of thy hands, give, that thou mayest labour for the redemption of thy sin; for "by alms and acts of faith sins are purged away." (Prov. xvi. 6; Dan.

5. Hall, *op. cit*, 20.

6. *The Apostolic Constitutions*, Book 8, 43, in Alexander Roberts and James Donaldson, editors, *Ante-Nicene Christian Library*, Vol. 17, *The Clementine Homilies, The Apostolic Constitutions* (Edinburgh, Scotland: T. & T. Clark, 1870), 252.

> iv. 27.) Thou shalt not grudge to give to the poor, nor when thou has given shalt thou murmur; for thou shalt know who will repay thee thy reward. For says he: "He that hath mercy on the poor man lendeth to the Lord; according to his gift, so shall it be repaid him again." (Prov. xix. 17.) Thou shalt not turn away from him that is needy; for says he: "He that stoppeth his ears, that he may not hear the cry of the needy, himself also shall call, and there shall be none to hear him." (Prov. xxi. 13.) Thou shalt communicate in all things to thy brother, and shalt not say *thy goods* are thine own; for the common participation of the necessaries of life is appointed to all men by God. Thou shalt not take off thine hand from thy son or from thy daughter, but shall teach them the fear of God from their youth; for says he: "Correct thy son, so shall he afford thee good hope." (Prov. xix. 18.)[7]

As soon as church buildings were erected, so too were libraries and schools; the schools accepted charity students.[8] Very early too the leaders of the early church asked the poor to stand before the church door to "provoke the most backward and inhuman soul to compassion."[9] Much stress was laid upon God's word that "none shall appear before me empty" (Ex. 23:15; 34:20). During Holy Week, prior to Easter, charitable works were increased; it was a time of rest and liberty for servants; many prisoners gained pardon and release, and all processes of law, criminal and civil, were suspended for the time being.[10]

It would be a mistake to assume that there was a uniform order over the centuries, because the faith at times waned seriously. All the same, the overall effects of Christian charity were remarkable. They still are. Whereas statist welfarism is impersonal and creates class hatreds because the citizens taxed

---

7. *Constitutions of the Holy Apostles*, Book 7, Sect. 12; in Alexander Roberts and James Donaldson, editors, *Ante-Nicene Fathers*, Vol. 7, *Lactantius, Venantius,* etc. (Grand Rapids, MI: Eerdmans, 1982 reprint) 468.

8. Joseph Bingham, *The Antiquities of the Christian Church*. Vol. 1 (London, England: Reeves and Turner, 1878), 313-14.

9. Ibid., 652-53.

10. Ibid., Vol. 2, 1187-8.

resent "giving" that is compulsory, and the recipients begin to resent their condition and to talk of "rights," Christian charity creates bonds and leads to changed lives. For example, I was given a letter yesterday by Ross Aiken of Murphys, California from a young woman who had been their tenant. She had not, eleven years before, been able to pay her rent and was a few months delinquent. Ross Aiken learned of the young woman's marital problem, that she was now alone and without transportation to go to work. He forgave her the rent, helped her, contacted Chalcedon, whose Deacon's Fund had enough for a good used car, and the woman gained her independence. Learning of Harriette Aiken's illness, on February 26, 1993, she (H.T.) wrote:

> Dear Harriette and Ross,
>
> Sure has been a long time! Most definitely another life time ago! Just wanted to thank you again for the kindness you both showed me when I was so lost. My life is great now, and *clean*! But without the great Christian people who showed faith in me when I had none along the way I'd have never made it! For being two of those people, thanks.
>
> I live in S. A., have been married 5 years in April. Have owned two gift stores (created). Now I have one here in S.A. A gift from the Lord. I sell unique and unusual gifts, books, lots of Christian stuff. I'm very happy. The kids are all so grown up! 12, 13, and 14 years old. Long way from the 1, 2, and 3 year olds you once had living in your house. But they are all very good kids! Thank God!
>
> Harriette, I hear you are not feeling well. I'll put you on the prayer list at St. Matthews. I hope you're feeling better. I have run a folk choir here; if you're ever down our way on Sunday, come by; we'll sing for you.

Long ago, St. John Chrysostom, a zealous promoter of Christian charity, made clear to his congregations that, however effective and far-ranging the charities of the diocese were, charity still begins at home with believing families.

In 1851, an American Protestant wrote *New Themes for the Protestant Clergy: Creeds without Charity, Theology without Humanity, Protestantism without Christianity.* The Reformation, he held, had clarified theology but progressively abandoned charity, and charity had long marked Christendom. He pleaded for a return to the great heritage of Christian charity. He rightly saw this as a lost heritage that needed to be reclaimed.

Unhappily, the very word *charity* has acquired meanings other than liberality towards the poor, the sick, the helpless, and the needy, which has been the meaning of Christian charity. Among the more common meanings of charity in recent generations is that moderate frame of mind which is neither indifference nor bigotry. Unhappily, even churchmen have stressed this meaning.[11] As the state took over welfare, the church retreated into Pietism, into concerns dealing mainly with the inner life of man. With this retreat came a spiritual poverty: men cannot neglect what God requires and still flourish. Proverbs 14:12, and 16:25 both tell us,

> There is a way which seemeth right unto a man, but the end thereof are the ways of death.

---

11. See B. D., "Charity not Indifference," in *The Orthodox Presbyterian*, Vol. 3 (Belfast, Ireland: William McComb, 1832), 96-102.

TWENTY-THREE

CHRISTIAN CHARITY

As we have seen, at one time Christian faith meant that the believer responded by actively working to bring God's grace and mercy to others, both by word and by deed. This meant the proclamation of the whole counsel of God, the redemption of the lost, the release of the bondage of those captive to sin, poverty, disease, and to various evils. In such thinking man was never the dead end of God's grace and mercy. The goal of God's redeeming power and grace was not man's soul but His Kingdom. Our Lord declares,

> 31. Therefore take no thought, saying What shall we eat? or, What shall we drink? or, Wherewithal shall we be clothed?
> 32. (For after all these things do the Gentiles seek:) for your heavenly Father knoweth that ye have need of all these things.
> 33. But seek ye first the kingdom of God, and his righteousness (or, justice); and all these things shall be added unto you. (Matt. 6:31–33)

These familiar words have an unfamiliar meaning. *First,* v. 31-32 restate v. 25: we are told there that we are not to trouble ourselves about food and clothing. God as our heavenly Father is aware of our needs. An egocentric concern is not God-honoring. *Second,* we must above all else be concerned with God's justice, and that justice or righteousness is clearly set before us in God's law-word. God's law commands justice, and this includes charity, for many of the laws require us to care for the needs of others. The helpless are our responsibility. Thus, charity is a personal and religious duty. *Third,* the Kingdom of God is our priority, not ourselves. Paul tells us, we are *not our own* (1 Cor. 6:19). We are God's servants, and we dare not expect God to serve our needs when we do not give Him His due, when we place our needs ahead of His Kingdom. *Fourth,* only as we take care of God's requirements will God take care of us. Only then will "all these things ... be added unto us."

Numerically, the church is very strong in our time. In actuality, it is very weak because the people of the church seek self-realization, social activities, an assurance that the question of heaven is resolved, and so on, all goals for the gratification of the believer.

It is true that the problems in the world around us are of staggering dimensions, but it has been our sin and dereliction which has created those problems, and God requires us to resolve them.

There was much preaching in the early church about charity or almsgiving. The New Testament Greek word *agape,* is translated often as *charity.* The Old English meaning of *charity* is love to God and love to man. The manifestation of *charity* in the life of man was seen as the presence of grace. When Paul in 1 Corinthians 13 spoke of *agape,* charity, or love, he understood the word in the active sense, as God's grace in us going out freely to others. He declared the three chief Christian graces to be faith, hope, and charity, or love, and the greatest of these is *agape,* charity.

We think now of bishops as administrators. They were originally pastors to pastors, and leaders in charity. Thus, Sidonius, in the course of thanking Bishop Patiens for his many good deeds, tells us this:

> It may be true that some of these good deeds are not peculiar to you, and are shared by colleagues; but there is one which is yours, as a first charge as lawyers say, and which even your modesty cannot deny; it is this, that when the Gothic ravages were over, and the crops were all destroyed by fire, you distributed wheat to the destitute throughout all the ruined land of Gaul at your own expense, though it would have been relief enough to our starving peoples if the wheat had come to them, not as a free gift, but by the usual paths of commerce. We saw the roads encumbered by your grain-carts. Along the Saone and Rhone we saw more than one granary which you had entirely filled … I cannot exactly tell the sum of gratitude which all the people owe you—inhabitants of Arles and Riez, Avignon, Orange, Viviers, Valence, and Trois Chateaux. It is beyond my power to count the total thanks of men who were fed without having to pay out a penny. But for the city of Clermont I can speak, and in its name I give you endless thanks; and all the more because your help had no obvious inducement: we did not belong to your province, no convenient waterway led to us, we had no money to offer. Measureless gratitude I give you on their behalf; they owe it to the abundant largess of your grain that they have now their own sufficiency once more.[1]

Christians replaced Roman imperial unity and concern with something far better, the universality of the church and of its concern in the name of Christ. This concern has been manifested in our century all over the world, in help, for example, to the Armenians in the 1915 massacres, but the imperative concern once shown has waned. At the time of Rome's fall, many churchmen with inherited wealth gave readily and heavily towards alleviating human need.[2] Many churchmen gained enduring respect for their charities, as witness Martin

---

1. Edward Motley Pickman, *The Mind of Latin Christendom* (London, England: Oxford University Press, 1937), 297-98.

2. Ibid., 311, note 57.

of Tours. In the medieval era, the monks were notable for their charities.

The early church had a major problem with the Roman Empire. For paganism, "the prime virtues were civic."[3] Christians challenged this and held that the prime virtues are God-centered. It is not the state that defines virtue but the triune God in His enscriptured word.

We today face a revival of classical statism. The locale of virtue is again the state, and Christianity is seen as a matter of personal choice, and its virtues as a matter of individual taste. The moral universe has been turned upside down. Where Christian charities are seen and noted, it is because of their seemingly humanitarian nature. The God-centered character of Christian charity is ignored. The *common ground* between peoples which is presented as the reason for concern for their welfare is their *common humanity.* But it is this common humanity which divides peoples. As fallen men, people hate one another, exploit, rob, and kill freely, and they are often never more apart than when brought together by statist action. A common humanity whose commonality is sin and evil shows more interest in exploitation than in mercy.

The theological foundation of Christian charity begins with Christ's atonement and His regenerating power, whereby we are made a new humanity, a new human race, in Jesus Christ. The grace we have received must go through us to others, both in a summons to redemption, and in acts of Christian help and mercy.

We are slow learners, and God is very patient with us. We were not made to please ourselves, nor was creation made for our glory. We are a people under orders, called into God's great army, and He has no patience with deserters. We must seek first His Kingdom and His justice (Matt. 6:33). We are not our own (1 Cor. 6:19), and we can never give priority to ourselves. To do so is to offend God, and who can stand before Him?

---

3. Ibid., 110.

TWENTY-FOUR

The Unknown John Calvin

An historian, Stephen A. McKnight, has called attention to the significance of Boccaccio's thinking as manifested in the first story of *The Decameron*. The setting is the plague of 1348. Seven ladies and three young men leave the city for the countryside to escape the plague. They retreat from the church and prayer because they see it as futile in the face of the plague. They entertain themselves with cynical stories about people *and* the church. The first story concerns a notary, a scoundrel, described as "belike the worst man that ever was born."[1] While visiting Burgundy on business, this man, Ciapperello da Prato, fell deathly ill. A cheat, a thief, a lecher, and a murderer, Ciapperello makes a radically false confession to a priest in which he appears to be a saintly man with a tender conscience. He concludes with a general statement of confession shrewdly intended as a manipulation of the rite in his favor. The naïve friar priest takes Ciapperello to be a saint, and he is buried in holy ground; miracles ensue at the grave of this "holy" man.

1. John Payne, translator, *The Decameron of Giovanni Boccaccio* (New York, NY: Triangle Books, [1931] 1940), 18.

McKnight pointed out that here and elsewhere Boccaccio developed "the key theme of appearance versus reality."[2] In fact, "Boccaccio's characters demonstrate that—at least on the human plane—appearance is reality."[3] Boccaccio, a priest, saw life as secular. He affirmed "the intrinsic value of secular existence." *The sacred and the secular are no longer essentially related by God's government and providence.* In fact, "The sacred does not disappear; there is still concern for salvation, but salvation seems to have little to do with everyday life."[4] We see this conclusion in men like Galileo, who limited the relevance of the Bible to salvation.[5] The Bible was no longer seen as governing the totality of life and thought but as limited to salvation and to providing a devotional manual. It was no longer seen as marching orders for all of life.

A new temper now prevailed, in Catholicism and in Protestantism later on. The Bible was viewed narrowly as a church manual and no more. Later on, in men like Bacon, Comte, and Marx, the new temper was developed further, according to McKnight:

> ...each writer's work displays the three primary characteristics of modernity: the consciousness of an epochal break with the past; a conviction that this break is due to an epistemological advance; and the belief that this new knowledge provides man the means of overcoming his alienation and regaining his true humanity.[6]

We can begin to see why Christianity is so impotent now. We live in a secularized world, where appearance *is* reality, and where Christianity is no longer seen as truly universal a faith but is limited to a concern for the afterlife. Biblical law is denied, and Calvinism is reduced to ideas about God and predestination whereas it is much more because it requires the

---

2. Stephen A. McKnight, *Sacralizing the Secular, The Renaissance Origins of Modernity* (Baton Rouge, LA: Louisiana State University Press, 1989), 31n.

3. Idem.

4. Ibid., 32.

5. Ibid., 37–38.

6. Ibid., 91.

government of all things by God and His law-word. It is an abandonment of Christianity not to see Jesus Christ as now and forever "the blessed and only Potentate, the King of kings, and Lord of lords" (1 Tim. 6:15). If Christ is not our King, then He is not our Priest nor Prophet. His offices are inseparable. How can He be our Prophet if He is not the absolute King, Lord, and Governor of all creation? And how can Christ be our great High Priest if He is not totally efficacious in His royal government of all things? Christianity no longer commands all things because it has been limited to a faith for the church rather than a faith for the world and for every sphere of life and thought. It has ceased to be universal or catholic, and catholicity does not mean control but a universality of total and efficacious relevance. A limited Christ is simply no Christ at all.

John Calvin sought to restore catholicity to the faith. As C. Gregg Singer observed, "Calvin found in the Scriptures the only adequate remedy for the human dilemma."[7] The charge of bibliolatry is often leveled against Calvin and his successors precisely because the Bible is the norm. As against the word of man, Calvinism affirms the word of God. As Singer noted, the problems faced by modern sociology exist "simply because modern America has neglected those basic Biblical principles which God has given for the guidance of His people."[8] Calvin held that, because God is God, all men are under the discipline of His moral law.[9] Calvin saw every aspect of the faith as very important. For example, he took the virtue of hospitality so seriously that he welcomed with joy strangers passing through Geneva.[10] This is an aspect of Calvin's life we must not forget. As a young man, Calvin left Noyon for Paris, at the risk

7. C. Gregg Singer, "Calvin and the Social Order," in Jacob T. Hoogstra, editor, *John Calvin, Contemporary Prophet* (Philadelphia, PA: Presbyterian and Reformed Publishing Company, 1959), 229.

8. C. Gregg Singer, *John Calvin, His Roots and Fruits* (Philadelphia, PA: Presbyterian and Reformed Publishing Company, 1967), 68.

9. Basil Hall, *John Calvin* (London, England: Routledge and Kegan Paul, [1956] 1962), 27.

10. Emanuel Stickelberger, *Calvin, A Life* (Richmond, VA: John Knox Press, 1954), 83.

of his life, to meet with Servetus in the hope of converting him. Servetus did not keep the appointment. Years later, when Servetus was a prisoner, Calvin reminded him of that episode.[11]

For Calvin, the kingship of Christ over all things was far more than a vague title. Commenting on Isaiah 9:6, "and the government shall be upon his shoulder," Calvin wrote,

> He therefore shows that the Messiah will be different from indolent kings, who leave off business and cares, and live at their ease; for he will be able to *bear the burden.* Thus he asserts the superiority and grandeur of his government, because by his own power Christ will obtain homage to himself, and he will discharge his office, not only with the tips of his fingers, but with his full strength.[12]

The kingship of Christ is a working rule. The Christian is called to extend the scope of the Kingdom into every realm. The early and medieval church had governed education, charity, and more. By Calvin's time, the cities had invaded these spheres, taking over the ownership of hospitals, orphanages, and so on. Such a situation prevailed in Geneva. Both with the help of the Council and without it, Calvin moved to a full ministry to human needs. Deacons were assigned to these duties: *hospitals* were an important area. A hospital then was housing for pilgrims, orphans, the elderly poor, the sick and others. Poor relief included those in and out of hospitals alike. Jobs were created for the healthy poor, who had to work to receive aid. At that time, the vagrancy problem in Europe was a major one because plague and war had destroyed the old patterns. The poor had to be cared for, according to Calvin, as a Christian duty.

We have two accounts of reformed worship, and its stress on alms:

---

11. R. N. Carew Hunt, *Calvin* (London, England: The Centenary Press, 1933), 47.

12. John Calvin, *Commentary on the Book of the Prophet Isaiah,* Vol. 1, (Grand Rapids, MI: Eerdmans, 1958), 308.

> (1551) He finishes the sermon, in the space of an hour, and, a prayer having been added, concludes. And first he admonished the church, if there are any worthy or necessary reasons—no doubt if there are marriages or baptisms, if any poor or sick person commends himself to the prayer of the church, and other things of the kind.
>
> Meanwhile two deacons walk about the whole church asking from each person alms for the use of the poor, but in silence, in order that they may not disturb the prayers. Thus they place before the eyes of each one a little bag hung on a long staff. And the same (deacons) stand at the door of the church, so that if those who were more intently attending to the prayers contributed nothing, they may give their alms in going out. [13]

Another account gives us a like report on the importance of charity in Calvinistic worship:

> Then, a psalm having been sung, the whole church is dismissed in peace by the preacher, with the commendation of the poor and the blessing, in these words: "Remember your poor and let each in turn pray for the others And may God have mercy on you and bless you. May the divine countenance shed His light upon you for the glory of His holy name, and keep you in His holy and saving peace. Amen"
>
> When, however, these things are said by the preacher, the deacons according to their turns must place themselves in order at the doors of the church, and after the church is dismissed, they diligently collect alms at the very doors of the church and immediately they write down whatever they have collected, in the church itself. Moreover, this is also customarily always observed in all the other gatherings of the church.[14]

The importance of the concluding clause cannot be stressed too much: "This is also customarily *always* observed in *all* the

---

13. Elsie Anne McKee, *John Calvin on the Diaconate and the Liturgical Almsgiving* (Geneva, Switzerland: Librairie Droz S.A., 1984), 39.
14. Ibid., 40.

other gatherings of the church." The charitable concern one for another marked all church meetings. Very obviously, the life of faith and the life of the church meant exactly what Paul said in Ephesians 4:25, "for we are members one of another."

This is an aspect of Calvin's thinking, and of the Reformed churches in those years and later, we seldom hear mentioned. Failure, however, to stress this aspect of Calvinism means to misunderstand it. It was not merely doctrine: it was faith and life inseparably connected.

Calvin himself answered the question, which are the reformed churches? with these words:

> Do we want to show that there is reformation among us? We must begin at this point, that is, there must be pastors who bear purely the doctrine of salvation, and then deacons who have the care of the poor.[15]

We hear routinely that the Reformed definition of a true church is one where the word is faithfully preached, the sacraments properly administered, and true discipline enforced. All this has its place, but Calvin gave an intensely practical definition:

> We saw this morning what position St. Paul discusses here, that is, that of those who in the ancient church were ordained to distribute the alms. It is certain that God wants such a rule observed in His church; that is, that there be care for the poor—and not only that each one privately support those who are poor, but that there be a public office, people ordained to have the care of those who are in need so that things may be conducted as they ought. And if that is not done, it is certain that we cannot boast that we have a church well-ordered and according to the gospel, but there is just so much confusion.[16]

Almsgiving was made a basic aspect of worship. Calvin saw both church and state under Christ's Kingship. He did not downgrade material things such as almsgiving. He held,

15. Ibid., 184.
16. Ibid., 183.

"From this we also gather that no form of life is more praiseworthy before God that than which yields usefulness to society."[17] In McKee's words, "Calvin goes beyond Luther in that his vision includes the restoration and renovation of the whole created order as its goal."[18] It is true that the Five Points of Calvinism do summarize doctrine of great importance to Calvin. It is also true that the three marks of a church can be found in Calvin. All the same, they give us a warped summary of Calvinism if we neglect the very great importance to Calvin of Christian charity, of being members one of another. To discuss Calvin without reference to his stress on the diaconate is like describing Switzerland with never a reference to the Alps. It can be accurate as far as it goes but still be false.

We have seen how Boccaccio replaced reality with appearance. This became the Renaissance view, and it is seen very clearly in Castiglione's *The Courtier.* Calvin's perspective was a plain and clear return to reality. Neither the ungodly nor the churchy are happy with it, but this is their loss in a fearful way.

17. Ibid., 119.
18. Ibid., 118.

TWENTY-FIVE

GOVERNMENT AND THE DIACONATE

(Reprinted from the *Chalcedon Report*, January 1995)

Over the years, I have repeatedly stressed the fact that it is a dangerous and potentially totalitarian fact to speak of *the state* as *the* government. The word *government* means many things. For us it must mean primarily the self-government of the Christian man as the *first* and basic sphere of government. If a man is not self-governing, then every other sphere of government is warped. The *second* sphere is the family, and its importance in Scripture is evident from beginning to end. The family is indeed the great nursery and training ground for all spheres of government, including and especially, self-government. *Third,* the church is a government, and like the family God-ordained. *Fourth,* the school is a government, as is, *fifth,* our vocation, which governs us daily. *Sixth,* a variety of private organizations, community relationships, and personal and family networks all govern us. Then, *seventh,* the state is a government, one form among many. In the English-speaking world, and in this country for generations, it was referred to as *civil government,* not government *per se.*

These spheres of government are in their fullness a product of Christianity. In most of the world, religion has been controlled by the state as a department thereof. For example, Rome allowed no unlicensed religion or god. The Roman Senate could make and unmake gods. No unlicensed groups, organizations, or meetings were permitted. Islam sees the state as the true church, and so on and on. The division of life into dependent, interacting spheres is an aspect of Biblical faith, with deep roots in the Old Testament.

This Biblical perspective is heightened by the fact of the tithe and the tax. According to Numbers 18:25–26, the Levites were to receive the tithe and then tithe a tenth part of the tithe to the priests. The care of the sanctuary and its music were given to the Levites, as were health, education, and charity. Deacons in the early church were called Levites because such areas were under their control. The civil tax, called an atonement or covering, protecting tax, was half a shekel, the same for all males aged twenty and over. Well into the medieval era *at least,* this tax was collected among Jews for civil purposes (Ex. 30:11–16). What this tells us is that neither church nor state was to be, under God's law, a powerful institution commanding society. The Levites, later deacons, had more extensive and diffuse duties. The Levites were not a centralized institution, but local ministers of God's grace and mercy.

The pattern is a clear one: a high degree of decentralization, with a strong emphasis on the individual and his family to govern in their spheres and to provide the necessary support to enable the Levites, or the deacons and their co-workers, to minister in God's Name.

We first meet deacons in the New Testament in Acts 6. The early church was practicing the Biblical care of the needy in its midst. The work became too much for the apostles, and seven deacons were chosen. The Levitical duties were thus given to a new order of Levites. These deacons not only cared for widows but also taught, and in Acts 7 we see Stephen as a powerful teacher of the faith. In Philippians 1:1, Paul addresses "the saints in Christ Jesus which are at Philippi, with the bishops and deacons." The deacons are clearly important in the Lord's service. In 1 Timothy 3:10–13, we see how similar the requirements for deacons are to those for bishops or presbyters:

> 10. And let these also first be proved; then let them use the office of a deacon, being found blameless.
> 11. Even so must their wives be grave, not slanderers, sober, faithful in all things.
> 12. Let the deacons be the husbands of one wife, ruling their children and their own houses well.
> 13. For they that have used the office of a deacon well purchase to themselves a good degree, and great boldness in the faith which is in Christ Jesus.

Perhaps, a good summary of deacons in the early centuries is that given by Schaff:

> The office of these deacons, according to the narrative in Acts, was to minister at the table in the daily love-feasts and to attend to the wants of the poor and the sick. The primitive churches were charitable societies, taking care of the widows and orphans, dispensing hospitality to strangers, and relieving the needs of the poor. The presbyters were the custodians, the deacons the collectors and distributors, of the charitable funds. To this work a kind of pastoral care of souls very naturally attached itself, since poverty and sickness afford the best occasions and the most urgent demand for edifying instruction and consolation. Hence, living faith and exemplary conduct were necessary qualifications for the office of deacon.
>
> Two of the Jerusalem deacons, Stephen and Philip, labored also as preachers and evangelists, but in the exercise of a personal gift rather than of official duty.
>
> In post-apostolic times, when the bishop was raised above the presbyter and the presbyter became priest, the deacon was regarded as Levite, and his primary function of care of the poor was lost in the function of assisting the priest in the subordinate parts of public worship and the adminis-

tration of the sacraments. The diaconate became the first of the three orders of the ministry and a stepping-stone of the priesthood. At the same time the deacon, by his intimacy with the bishop as his agent and messenger, acquired an advantage over the priest.[1]

There is no adequate history of the diaconate, but one fact in its history deserves both attention and revival. Just as the presbyter's calling is a full-time ministry, so too the deacon's service requires a full-time commitment. As the church revives and strengthens the diaconate and makes it a vocation for those called to it so too will the church grow and society become steadily Christianized. Nothing is clearer from Acts than the fact that the seven deacons were not part-time workers but full-time servants of Christ. The Christian Levites were the functioning grace and mercy of Christ's Kingdom. The deacons revealed clearly that Christ's Kingdom is indeed a government. The works of charity carried on by the deacons were in marked contrast to the costly and evil welfarism of Rome. At times, this made deacons a special target of persecution because their work not only manifested Christ's royal government but also His grace and mercy.

We today face the coming collapse of the welfare state and its programs, all of which have helped destroy the recipients of statist welfare. As our modern Rome faces collapse, we need to revive the diaconate in its holy and necessary calling.

All this leads in one direction and to one conclusion: *We must take government back from the state and restore it to Jesus Christ.* The *government* in every sphere of life and thought *must be* and shall be upon His shoulder (Isa. 9:6). Because He is the blessed and only Potentate, the King of kings, and the Lord of lords (1 Tim. 6:15), nothing can be withheld from His rule. He has said, "*All power* is given unto me in heaven and in earth" (Matt. 28:18), and I therefore find it baffling that

1. Philip Schaff, *History of the Christian Church,* Vol. 1, (New York: NY: Charles Scribner's Sons, 1882), 499-500.

churchmen who profess to believe the Bible prefer their political party to God's Christ and to God's law.

The church has confused worship with Christianity. The church is a barren place if it be no more than a worship center. It must be the training center, the barracks building of God's army, where Christ's people are prepared to exercise dominion in those spheres of life which surround them.

A letter I received a few days ago from a young man in the deep South very clearly raises an issue which is critically important for our time. He wrote in part:

> I have a Christian roommate who maintains an eschatology that pre-tribulation dispensationalism is proven to be the only end-time occurrence according to Scripture.
>
> I told him I was a reconstructionist post-millennialist of the Augustinian school of teaching, that I thought the Church of Jesus Christ would prevail in real time. I do not believe in a pre-tribulation rapture.
>
> My roommate said I was a heretic and all post-millennialists are heretics.
>
> Do you have any advice for me? He also said that a professing Christian need not lead a holy life to be saved. He just makes a profession of faith on the spot and he gets zapped with the Holy Spirit and he is saved just like that.
>
> What is your opinion of the above?[2]

Such thinking is commonplace. Sadly, many who are neither Arminian nor dispensationalist pre-millennialists have come to believe that a bare confession of faith is binding on God but not on them. Such positions may *appeal* to the Bible, but they are not *governed* by the word of God.

I began by calling attention to the fact that we today falsely equate *government* with the state, or civil government. At times over the centuries the church or some of the churches have

2. Letter, in part, of September 1994.

sought to equate government with the *state.* If Isaiah 9:6, Matthew 28:18, and many other texts are right, we must equate government with our Lord, Jesus Christ. He is Priest, Prophet, and King.

As our great High Priest, He has made atonement for us, intercedes for us, and prays for us. As the great Prophet, He speaks God's clear and infallible word to us. As King, He is our ruler and our lawgiver. If we look elsewhere for any of these things, we are faithless, because other lords have then had dominion over us (Isa. 26:13).

When other lords have dominion over us, the Lord God gives us over into captivity to our enemies. He will not defend nor bless those who will not have Him as their King. This is why we are in the state we are in. The question then is "Why speak ye not a word of bringing the King back?" (2 Samuel 19:10).

TWENTY-SIX

CHARITY AND THE STATE

Some years ago, I was at a dinner for pastors and priests, called to give them an opportunity to hear an internationally noted economist. The generally humorous table talk before the man spoke was church talk. A priest said that a well-known fact among priests was that no one ever confessed to being stingy. We laughed at that, and others recounted their similar observations, all too true. I have heard too many laymen say that the clergy is money hungry and misuses the funds given. But when asked, if you are provided with a list of fiscally responsible churches and Christian causes, *will you give?* they are irritated at the question. Stinginess rules them.

Today, in the mid-1990s, we are told that the giving by Americans to all causes runs between two and three percent, obviously not a tithe. If it be said that this includes Christians and non-Christians alike, the fact remains that the non-Christian giving to humanistic causes rivals specifically Christian giving. Christians do not put their money where their mouth is. The Christian retreat from the church is one of the catastrophes of history.

The churches, moreover, have become in essence socialistic rather than Christian. One area after another has been surrendered to the state. God's law *requires* that His people govern through education, health provisions, and works of charity, among other things. The surrender of these areas to the state has been steady and revolutionary. Pietism and Arminianism were the motivating forces in the church's surrender, and the desire for power an aspect of the state's motivation.

It can and must be said that too often the continuing Christian charities have been maintained with statist funds. William Tucker, among others, has called attention to the fact that various Christian causes depend heavily on statist financial support. Catholic Charities are the largest non-profit organization in the United States. In 1993, of its $1.9 billion budget, $1.2 billion, sixty-five percent, came from statist sources. Volunteers of America raised $25 million but received $198 million, or sixty-nine percent of its $289 million budget from city, state, and federal contracts. According to *Non-Profit Times*, in 1993, reported Tucker, the one hundred largest non-profit funding organizations received twenty-two percent of their income from statist sources. Lutheran Social Ministries did not qualify for the *Non-Profit Times* list because they did not get even ten percent from charitable gifts; they received ninety-two percent of their income from the state. Of all the tax-exempt organizations, hospitals, colleges, and other religious groups, about one million groups, c. 550,000 are charities. These raised c. $100 billion in goods and services in 1993; of this $50 billion came from individuals, $10 billion from corporations, foundations, and bequests, and another $40 billion primarily from statist sources. Such groups oppose balanced budget amendments. Not all non-profits will take state funds. Some major groups listed by Tucker include Shriners Hospitals for Crippled Children, United Jewish Appeal, YMCA of U. S. A., American Cancer Society, Christian Children's Fund, National Benevolent Association Christian Church, Muscular Dystrophy Association, and the United Negro College Fund.[1]

1. William Tucker, "Sweet Charity," *The American Spectator*, February, 1995, 38-41.

The state too often has been ready to do what the church has indifferently surrendered. The results have been seriously derelict. Bogdanovich has shown what religious, private, and statist hospitals have done to defraud state agencies of money.[2]

The growth of statist power in health, education, and welfare has been marked by a retreat of Christians from those sectors. This has enabled the state to enter by default into society's key area of power, the family. Control of the family means control over all of society. The church cannot be strong where the family is weak. The decay of family and church is the decay of society.

Complaints against the growing power of the state are increasingly in evidence. They are well grounded, but their fallacy is that they are simply complaints, not remedial action. The power to alter society is essentially in the hands of the people, but it is a serous fallacy to assume that the *primary* power possessed by the people is the vote, agitation, protests, demonstrations, or the like. As the constituent and most important unit in society, it is the person who can most alter it by changing himself, governing his family, tithing, establishing or aiding independent Christian agencies in society, and so on.

The state reflects past changes, not present ones. It rests on public consent (or indifference), and because it is governed in the twentieth century by public opinion, it moves commonly with glacial slowness.

Once Attorney General of the United States, Herbert Brownell, in an interview not too long after World War II, said that "all of the great administrative improvements in New York in recent years came through the efforts of laymen. Citizens forced judges and lawyers to make changes ... It has to be laymen. They're the people who are hurt by the malfunctions

2. Walt Bogdanovich, *The Great White Lie* (New York: NY: Simon Schuster, 1991).

of the courts."[3] The malfunctions of society most affect the people, and they are the ones who must correct them.

This means that the starting point of all reformation is the individual and his relationship to the triune God. The old proverb is true: You cannot make a good omelet with bad eggs; neither can a good society be established on bad persons. To expect society to be moral when it is made up of immoral men is an illusion, one of the major illusions of the twentieth century.

One of the major shifts, a revolutionary one, occurred early in the twentieth century. It was a change whose origins were in the Enlightenment, but which, in the United States, became clearly visible in the 1920s, and educators had a major part in it. According to Robert Nisbet, the church was once "the most widely accepted institutional base for reform of society," but educators, social scientists, and philosophers in the 1920s put "full emphasis on the national state" as the key agency. John Dewey was very influential in this shift. In terms of this school of thought, "the state would be the tireless champion of the people, as against the varied factions of business, religion, and ordinary politics."[4] In our time, humanistic, statist law is seen "as the most potent force for social change now imaginable."[5]

A major aspect of this change has been the erosion of morality and authority. God's transcendent and unchanging law is denied. Statist law changes *daily*. No man can now know all the law and all its ramifications. The result is the rise of anarchy, and the erosion of law is basic to it. We are again in an era comparable to that of the Hebrew judges, when God was rejected as King, and "every man did that which was right in his own eyes" (Judges 21:25).

---

3. Howard James, *Crisis in the Courts* (New York, NY: David McKay, [1967] 1968), 207.

4. Robert Nisbet, *The Present Age, Progress and Anarchy in Modern America* (New York, NY: Harper & Row, 1988), 65.

5. Ibid., 67.

Only those who lived in the era of the New Deal and President Franklin Delano Roosevelt can appreciate the extent to which he was a messianic figure. To be critical of him was to invite hostility and a fistfight from other students, and, from teachers, the accusation that one was rich, an "economic royalist"!

Nisbet singled out Jean-Jacques Rousseau (1712-1778) as "the man of the hour" in twentieth century American history. Rousseau, who declared Plato to be his greatest teacher, "transferred, as it were, grace from the body of the church to the body of the state, the state based upon the social contract and the general will."[6]

Rousseau, in *The Social Contract,* in effect called for the divinization of the state as the new source of grace *and law,* because he held, "only Gods can give laws to men."[7] The Legislator is thus an "extraordinary" figure in the state.[8] Hence, Rousseau held,

> Whoso would undertake to give institutions to a People must work with full consciousness that he has set himself to change, as it were, the very stuff of human nature; to transform each individual who, in isolation, is a complete but solitary whole, into a part of something greater than himself, from which, in a sense, he derives his life and his being; to substitute a communal and moral existence for their purely physical and independent life with which we are all of us endowed by nature. His task, in short, is to take from a man his own proper powers, and to give him in exchange powers foreign to him as a person, which he can use only if he is helped by the rest of the community. The more complete the death and destruction of his natural powers, the greater and more durable will those be which he acquires, and the more solid and perfect will that community be of which he forms a part. So true is this that the

---

6. Ibid., 55.

7. Jean-Jacques Rousseau, *The Social Contract,* Book 2, Chapter 7, in Sir Ernest Barker, *Social Contract, Essays by Locke, Hume, and Rousseau* (London, England: Oxford University Press, [1947], 1958), 291.

8. Ibid., 292.

> citizen by himself is nothing and can do nothing, save with the co-operation of his neighbours, and the power acquired by the whole is equal or superior to the sum of the powers possessed by its citizens regarded as natural men. When that result has been achieved, and only then, can we say that the art of legislation has reached the highest stage of perfection of which it is capable.[9]

This is a remarkable statement on the state as the new god. Rousseau, as a native of Geneva, the home once of Calvinism, knew that conversion means the remaking of human nature from its fallen estate in Adam to a new creation in the last Adam, Jesus Christ (1 Cor. 15:45–50). "To change, as it were, the very stuff of human nature," was a divine act of grace before Rousseau; now it was an act of state. For membership in Christ's new human race Rousseau substituted membership in the modern state. In Christ, the old man in us, the fallen Adam, must die to make way for the new man. For Rousseau, there must be a thoroughly "complete … death and destruction of his (man's) natural powers" in order to make him truly a good citizen of his community. In himself man "is nothing"; only in the state, the social contract, can he be anything.

What for the Christian community, in its acts of mercy and charity, was an expression of grace is, in the state, an aspect of the life of the bureaucracy. Christian charity is a personal act; statist welfare is impersonal and bureaucratic.

There is another and central aspect to this problem. In Scripture, man's basic problem is original sin, the will to be one's own god, "knowing," or determining for oneself, what is good and evil, right and wrong, law and morality (Gen. 3:5). This is not only the meaning of sin but also of madness. In madness, self-will takes over, and the desire to gain one's way predominates. "My will be done" becomes law. Madness like sin insists on replacing reality with one's own delusions and wishes.

---

9. Jean-Jacques Rousseau, "The Social Contract," Book 2, Chapter 7, Barker, ibid., 291-92.

The modern state sees itself as man's savior, as capable of resolving problems in various spheres of man's life. Its failures are seen as trial runs and stepping stones to truth or the resolution of problems. The growth of the state is into illusions and self-deceptions as its answers to problems create only bigger problems. The proliferation of statist answers leads to an increase in new problems and to social unrest. The welfare state has become the source of legalized abortion and euthanasia. The more the modern state sins, the more virtuous it feels because it is transgressing the law of the old God. In this it resembles Victor Hugo, who once wrote in a letter to Victor Pavie, on July 25, 1833:

> I have committed more transgressions than ever this year, and I have never been a better person. I am much better now than in my days of *innocence,* which you miss. Before I was innocent; now I am indulgent. That's a progress, God knows. At my side is my dear, sweet companion, an angel who also knows this, whom you venerate as I do, who forgives me, who loves me. Love and forgiveness, they are not of man but of God—or woman.[10]

In more ways than one, Victor Hugo reflected the modern mentality.

---

10. Eugene Ionesco, *Hugoliad, or the Grotesque and Tragic life of Victor Hugo* (New York, NY: Grove Press, 1987), 116.

TWENTY-SEVEN

THE HUMANIST REVOLUTION

In 1973, John D. Rockefeller III published his book *The Second American Revolution, Some Personal Observations.* The revolution was from Christianity to humanism as the basis of American culture. Of course, Rockefeller avoided all reference to Orthodox Judaism and Biblical Christianity except a vague one. Clearly too, he rejected the idea of God's determination of all things. "History is not predetermined by some random pattern or unknown force. *It will be determined by us.*"[1] This is a logical conclusion on Rockefeller's part, given his thoroughly humanistic premises. As between God and man, he clearly chooses man and wants no part of the Biblical God.

His premises are clearly stated. *First,* "we are all members of the same human family."[2] This seems to be an obvious fact, but we must see it in context. Rockefeller's faith is not in God but in man, in people.[3] The Christian view is that there are two races on earth, two kinds of people, on the one hand the old

1. John D. Rockefeller, III, *The Second American Revolution* (New York, NY: Harper & Row, 1973), 51.
2. Ibid., 25.
3. Ibid., 34.

fallen human race born of Adam, sinful and at war with God, and, on the other, the new humanity born again in the last Adam, Jesus Christ. This means that man is not created by God but has evolved and is "a social animal."[4] Because there is no Fall for Rockefeller, men everywhere manifest good will.

Then, *second,* because of humanism, new and better values are emerging. These include a positive view of nature. This too is logical: if God is dropped, man's source for positive values will be either nature or man. Thus, Rockefeller sees as an emerging value "a positive view of human nature." Man is seen as inherently good rather than evil. If we adopt this positive view, this will "encourage the emergence of this inherent goodness." Next, "a sense of community" is one of the new values, based on man's being a social animal. Individuality, freedom, and equality are also cited. Rockefeller is blissfully ignorant of Tocqueville's *Democracy in America* and its thesis that equality destroys freedom and individuality. Next come democracy, social responsibility, and "authority in status in perspective." His comments reflect his isolation from the real world of New York. Then he cites as emerging values "materialism in perspective" and "a positive view of work." Did Christian society previously lack these? Has not the work ethic declined with the rise of humanism?

Another emerging value is a "positive view of sexuality." No connection is made between morality and sexuality. When Rockefeller wrote, "the sexual revolution" was well under way; was this an emerging value? Then he cites "the interdependence of man." By this he does not mean Christian community but an emerging world order.

"A metaphysical or religious consciousness" as an emerging value refers to "Eastern religions, mysticism, extrasensory perception, the occult in general, and ... existentialism and other transcendental philosophies," i.e., to everything non-Christian.[5]

---

4. Ibid., 182.
5. Ibid., 41–49.

Third, the Second American Revolution is towards "a giving society."[6] Of course, Rockefeller's Second American Revolution has led to a decrease in charitable giving, but what he has in mind is statist welfarism. Humanism has made us a taking society, and semantic tricks cannot obscure that fact.

Not surprisingly, Rockefeller has a chapter on "The Politics of Humanism." Humanism is for welfare, not charity, and it creates not community, but a power state. Rockefeller was proud when his son Jay entered politics in West Virginia. His ideas are implicitly socialistic, and he speaks favorably of a "planning society."[7] His work echoes all the favorite myths of humanism, including overpopulation, a concern of humanists from Plato's day to the present. The world is always overpopulated if there are people in it ones dislikes. Humanistic reformers and revolutionaries have usually sought to eliminate their unwanted peoples, often very brutally.

Welfarism is a means of buying off potentially troublesome peoples. Its goals are not for the good of the people but for the good of the state and its elite leaders. As a result, statism is anti-charity. The Soviet Union regarded charity as counterrevolutionary because it made Christianity and its charity the hope of the people.

The humanist revolution is thus emphatically anti-charity. Since its goal is to control man and society, it is intolerant of all influences contrary to its hope. Basic to Christianity is the fact that it is called to advance the Kingdom of God. This has priority. In our Lord's words, "seek ye first the kingdom of God, and his righteousness" (or, justice) (Matt. 6:33). The humanist revolution of Rockefeller *et al.* is at war with Christianity, no less so than the French and Russian Revolutions, or any other revolution. We cannot cope with our world and its problems if we do not recognize who is at war with us.

---

6. Ibid., 113.
7. Ibid., 143-163.

TWENTY-EIGHT

Work and Charity

Too much modern thinking is governed by a lack of systematic thinking; this is especially true of churchmen and conservatives who seem to prefer a smorgasbord assortment of ideas. Churchmen, for example, routinely drop Biblical laws and doctrines which seem to them likely to offend the modern (or post-modern) mind. This rejection of sound thinking marks the so-called post-moderns most of all because their rejection of meaning is a radical one. Ultimately, to reject meaning is to reject life; if life and death are equally meaningless, then life has been rejected.

The German Christian Reconstructionist leader and scholar, Dr. Thomas Schirrmacher, has called attention to an important aspect of the Biblical revelation. The Bible reveals the God who works, Schirrmacher has pointed out very tellingly. Work is not a burden nor a curse, although Genesis 3:17–19 tells us that man's sin brings a curse to all his activities, especially to work, which should be man's most positive endeavor. Man, in working, is both obedient to and imitative of God, so that work is essential to man's welfare and progress.

Webster's Second International Dictionary, unabridged, gives almost a page to defining *work,* but it is not a Biblical definition. Work preceded the fall of man, and is not a product of sin nor the fall. In the Garden of Eden, man had work to do, to cultivate, prune, and keep the Garden, and also the scientific task of "naming" or classifying the animals (Gen. 2:15, 20). The Garden of Eden was a restricted area wherein man was to learn how to exercise dominion and to subdue the earth (Gen. 1:26–28). Eden was a pilot project for the conversion of the whole earth into the Kingdom of God by man's obedient service to the triune God.

Work thus from the beginning is a religious function and a central one. By means of work, man must turn the earth into the glorious realm God requires it to be. It is therefore anti-Christian to regard work as a punishment, or something to be avoided. On February 16, 1995, in a bank in Angels Camp, California, I saw a man, younger than myself, perhaps sixty-seven years old, with a cap that bore these words: "Eat your heart out, I'm retired." Not too many years ago, men were going to court to file lawsuits against compulsory retirement.

In the student rebellions of the 1960s, student revolutionaries at the University of California at Berkeley saw the necessity for work as a capitalist conspiracy and they insisted that a work-free world was possible.

The flight from work is often a flight from God, and from what He requires of us. Because man wants to be his own god (Gen. 3:5), he wants a fiat world where his own word is creative and determinative. Thus, Paul's requirement in 2 Thessalonians 3:10 is seen by many as grossly inhumane in holding,

> For even when we were with you, this we commanded you, that if any would not work, neither should he eat.

This is a requirement, *first,* that no able-bodied person live off the charity of others. Rome was the great empire of the day; Paul was a citizen thereof, and Rome's wealth was being slowly eroded by its welfarism. "Bread and circuses" was the order of the day. *Second,* because Scripture declares work to be God-given and a calling from Him and in Him, refusal to work is an act of religious rebellion against God's order, not a light matter. Work is too basic to God's order for man to avoid it or to downgrade it. A culture which treats work as a burden, or something to be avoided, is anti-Christian. *Third*, work is essential to the maintenance and advancement of society: no work, no future.

The *Apostolic Constitutions*, dated by some in the fourth century, show us the continuity of St. Paul's requirement in 2 Thessalonians 3:10. In Book 2, Section 8, the title for the section is, "On the Duty of Working for a Livelihood."[1]

The anti-work attitude was endemic to paganism. Paul, in 1 Corinthians, tells us that some or many in the Corinthian Church saw themselves as kings, as outside and above the law in Christ, and as a people above work. Paul tells them that he labors with his own hands (1 Cor. 4:8–13). The Gnostics, as their ideas developed, showed themselves to be anti-work, and they regarded the working God as inferior to their idle god.[2] How insanely these Gnostics were against work appears in their view of 1 Corinthians 4:12, where Paul speaks of working with his own hands. The Gnostics held that Paul here referred, not to manual labor, but to masturbation.[3]

As against this, the Biblical position stressed work and charity. Julian the Apostate had learned of the views of Jews and Christians, and he tried to reform paganism accordingly. He observed, "no Jew ever has to beg, and the impious Galileans [Christians][4] support not only their own poor but ours as well." Tertullian spoke of the Christian virtue of charity and contrasted it to Roman welfarism wherein the welfare recipient gained his grants by threatening men and society.

---

1. "Constitution of the Holy Apostles," in *Ante-Nicene Fathers*, Vol. 7 (Grand Rapids, MI: Eerdmans, 1982 reprint), 424.

2. Robert M. Grant, *Early Christianity and Society* (San Francisco, CA: Harper & Row, 1977), 68.

3. Ibid., 69. Grant's sources for this are Epiphanius, *Haer* XXVI, 11, 1-2; of Clement, *Exc. Ex Theod* 49, 1; Irenaeus, *Adv. Haer* I, 5, 3; Hyppolytus, *Ref.* VI, 33; 34:8; Heracleon in Origin, *Ioh. Comm.*, XII, 50.)

4. Ibid., 125.

> But also to every one who asks me I will give on the plea of charity, not under any intimidation. Who asks? He says. But he who uses intimidation does not ask. One who threatens if he does not receive, does not crave, but compels. It is not alms he looks for, who comes not to be pitied, but to be feared. I will give, therefore, because I pity, not because I fear, when the recipient honours God and returns me his blessing; not when rather he both believes that he has conferred a favour on me, and beholding his plunder, says, "Guilt money."[5]

But modern welfarism is too often guilt money. The poor, whether undeserving or deserving, too commonly try to make prospective donors feel guilty, so that much giving is a form of bribery. The state grants of welfare are gained at times by threats of rioting, and crowds of welfare recipients have at times staged demonstrations and entered political offices, as in the infamous incident in New York State in Governor Nelson Rockefeller's offices.

It is true that Christian charity can be and has been abused. The cynical Lucian, the Roman satirist, gives us an example of a pretended Christian prophet, Peregrinus, exploiting even the poorer Christians and widows and orphans by making himself into a martyred man in his imprisonment.[6] Such incidents are a relatively minor episode when compared to the massive deceptions and frauds in statist charity.

Turning again to 2 Thessalonians 3:10, Paul's command that those who will not work must not be fed had an explicit injunction against feeding those who refuse to be a part of the working world, and, like those Tertullian spoke of, want to live by intimidating the workers. Implicit in Paul's works is the Biblical requirement of charity to widows and orphans, and to all who for one valid reason or another cannot find work or are unable to find work. Those who work have, *first,* a duty to refuse support and food to the deliberate non-workers, and

---

5. Tertullian, "De Fuga in Persecutione," 13, in *The Ante-Nicene Fathers,* Vol. 4 (Grand Rapids, MI: Eerdmans, 1982 reprint), 124.

6. Lucian, *Works,* Vol. 5, Sec. 12.18 (Cambridge, MA: Harvard University Press, [1936] 1962), 13.

second, a duty to help all the truly needy with their bounty, great or small, which results from their work. This means that both the workers and the needy are oriented to a world of work whose goal is a Christian society.

"The communion of the saints" is an article of faith. An early English form of the Apostles' Creed renders it "Of the saints, the society." The purpose of Biblical charity is the creation of a godly society. The majority will be workers, but the society must include the needy as well.

In the first century before Christ, a Jewish sage, Shema'iah said simply, "Love work."[7] The early church held to this same premise, as witness Paul. The advantage of a Biblical culture is its views on work and charity.

7. Grant, *op.cit.*, 66-67.

TWENTY-NINE

JUSTICE AND CHARITY

In Hebrew, there are three words based on a common root, the word *justice.* "*Tzaddik* is a righteous person; *tsedek* is justice in a court of law; *tsedakah* is 'charity.'"[1] Because God is the Creator and Lawgiver, in His sovereign purpose and plan the just or righteous man, the court of law, and charity are essentially related.

These three concepts manifest themselves in God's law. The sabbatical laws, such as the seventh year rest, have among their purposes, charity. According to Exodus 23:10–11,

> 10. And six years thou shalt sow thy land, and shalt gather in the fruits thereof:
> 11. But the seventh year thou shalt let it rest and lie still; that the poor of thy people may eat: and what they leave the beasts of the field shall eat. In like manner thou shalt deal with thy vineyard, and with thy oliveyard.

---

1. Rabbi Meir Zlotowitz, Rabbi Nosson Scherman, *Bereishis, Genesis,* Vol. 1 (Brooklyn, NY: Mesorah Publications, [1977] 1980), 198.

The tithe for the poor, and the cancellation of debts, also have the needy in mind. The laws of charity are many. *The whole of the law expresses the nature of God,* and this is most certainly true of the laws of charity. If we are without charity, we are without faith because we then fail to recognize the grace, mercy, and charity of God towards us. In Deuteronomy 10:16–19, we are told,

> 16. Circumcise, therefore, the foreskin of your heart, and be no more stiffnecked.
> 17. For the LORD your God is God of gods, and Lord of lords, a great God, a mighty, and a terrible, which regardeth not persons, nor taketh reward:
> 18. He doth execute the judgment of the fatherless and widow, and loveth the stranger, in giving him food and raiment.
> 19. Love ye therefore the stranger: for ye were strangers in the land of Egypt.

The force of this statement is not at once apparent unless we see that God says that they are not to be like the Egyptians, contemptuous of alien and weaker peoples. God, Who is the omnipotent and transcendent One, is not only terrifying in His Person, but also very mindful of widows and orphans, and He *loves* the aliens. "Charity is an attribute of God Himself."[2]

A strong or virtuous woman is one who "stretcheth out her hand to the poor; yea, she reacheth forth her hands to the needy" (Prov. 31:20). It is the character of God to be charitable, and also of men and women who are the Lord's.

Over the centuries, Jews, in terms of the law, cared for the poor. Since in the Christian era the old order was gone, "charity wardens" in every Jewish community took care of all needs. These were analogous to the Christian diaconate, which had the same responsibility. Among the Jews, the charity normally took four forms: 1) money; 2) gifts of various kinds; 3) clothing; and 4) burial. The Christian deacons

---

2. Haim Hillel Ben-Sasson, "Charity," in *Encyclopaedia Judaica,* Vol. 5 (Jerusalem, Israel: Keter Publishing Company, 1971) 339.

included also education, health care, relief and aid to abused women, the care of the elderly and of orphans, and like matters. Jewish charitable organizations took care of like needs. The scope of Jewish charities has expanded in the twentieth century.

We have seen that *justice* and *charity* are essentially related. *Zedek* is justice, as is *zedakah*. Because Scripture consistently links justice to mercy and grace, in time Judaism came to see *zedakah* as meaning charity. This meant at the same time that justice came to mean love. Since both express the nature of God, they are essentially related and are inseparable. Man errs in opposing law, justice, and charity against one another. "Man is obliged to imitate God by acting on the principle of compassionate equity and—at the final consummation of history—justice and mercy become identical."[3]

There is an important aspect of Hebrew and Jewish charity that must not be overlooked. "Even the recipient of charity is required to give charity."[4]

In Mark 12:41–44, we see an example apparently of such giving:

> 41. And Jesus sat over against the treasury, and beheld how the people cast money into the treasury: and many that were rich cast in much.
> 42. And there came a certain poor widow, and threw in two mites, which make a farthing.
> 43. And he called unto him his disciples, and saith unto them, Verily I say unto you, That this poor widow hath cast more in, than all they which have cast into the treasury:
> 44. For all they did cast in of their abundance; but she of her want did cast in all that she had, even all her living.

This account is a fair one: we are told that the "rich cast in much." These were not tithes but free-will offerings for the Temple. The widow did not feel that poverty made her ex-

---

3. Steven S. Schwarzschild, "Justice," in Ibid., Vol. 10, 476f.

4. "Charity," in Geoffrey Wigoder, editor, *Encyclopedic Dictionary of Judaism* (Jerusalem, Israel: Keter Publishing House, 1974) 120.

empt from the moral obligation of giving. Our Lord *deliberately watched* how people gave. We have no reason to believe He is less observant of us.

Religion is either man-centered or God-centered, and non-Christian, non-Biblical faiths are men-centered. The concern of pagans, whether in the church or out of it, whether in an ancient mystery religion or in a modern church, is man-centered. In effect, the believer is interested in what God can do for him or her. As against this, Biblical faith insists that justice means righteousness in us, set forth by our faithfulness to God's law; because God's law is the expression of His nature and being, to believe in God means to obey His law and to manifest His communicable attributes, which include grace, mercy, and charity. To believe in God means to establish our courts on His law. Moreover, to believe in God is to know His grace, mercy, and charity to us in and through Jesus Christ, His atonement, and His providential care.

The Hebrew term for charity has as its context God's covenant with His people. It is therefore essentially linked not only with the righteous man and with courts of God's law, but with God's covenant. To be charitable is to be faithful and grateful to God for His covenant. It is a covenantal response. The New Testament Greek commonly uses *eleos,* compassion, mercy, and pity, for the same concept. In the Septuagint, *eleos* is commonly used to indicate the same concept, but *eleos* has a different reference. Esser saw the Greek word's background as "predominantly psychological." However, this stress has as its purpose the avoidance of mere outward compliance to the letter of the law in order that the believer might fulfill its spirit by stressing the inner requirement. Esser called attention to the fact that Paul had received mercy (*eleethen*) in order that he might become an apostle. The Lord's mercy (*eleemenos*) had made Paul trustworthy and faithful to the covenant.

James 2:13 reads, "For he shall have judgment without mercy (*aneleos*), that hath shewed no mercy (*eleos*); and mercy (*eleos*) rejoiceth against judgment."[5] James' statement is insep-

---

5. H. H. Esser, "Mercy," in Colin Brown, General Editor, *The New International Dictionary of New Testament Theology,* Vol. 2 (Grand Rapids, MI: Zondervan, 1976), 594-598.

arable from the Hebrew understanding of charity. Those who are merciful or charitable manifest the Gospel faith, and they will triumph in the times of judgment: they have been faithful to the covenant. Our Lord tells us, "by their fruits ye shall know them" (Matt. 7:20). Paul tells us that Christ frees us from sin to make us the servants of *righteousness* (Rom. 6:18), and the word used is *dikaiosune*, right action (Matt. 6:33). Matthew 6:1–33 gives us the meaning of this righteousness. When Matthew 6:1 tells us, "Take heed that ye do not your alms before men, to be seen of them" the word *alms* is in the Greek *dikaiosune*, righteousness. Without charity, there is no righteousness because *grace to us results in grace in us towards others.* Charity does not save us, but if we are saved, we are charitable. This is what the parable of the last judgment is about: "Inasmuch as ye did it not to one of the least of these, ye did it not unto me" (Matt. 25:45). At this point, Judaism and Roman Catholicism have been sometimes more faithful than many Protestants who, by assuming that their doctrine was right, felt exempted from the requirements by faith.

It is a fearful offense to separate doctrines in the Bible, to assume that law and grace, mercy and justice, love and judgment, and much, much more, can be opposed one to another. Men should not dare to put asunder what God has joined together.

THIRTY

"Pure Religion and Undefiled"

The origin of the word *define* is in the Latin *de finere*, to limit, to set a boundary, an end. Definitions thus establish boundaries to words and things. Language would be impossible if there were no limits on the meanings of word. Definitions are propositional truths; they set forth the boundaries of meanings for words and things.

The concept of *definition* is a religious one. How we establish limits and boundaries depends on our religious presuppositions. Thus, the artist Marcel Duchamp, militantly against Christian faith and morality, was also against meaning. "His work was meant for none but himself, and he took every precaution to see that nothing of it should be intelligible to an outsider."[1] He believed that "the concept of judgment should be abolished."[2] For years, "the creation of a new language was to be one of his principal preoccupations."[3] The task was, of course, an impossible one. How could a new language avoid

1. Robert Lebel, *Marcel Duchamp* (New York: NY: Grove Press, 1959) 69.
2. Ibid., 56.
3. Ibid., 26.

meaning? The definition of a word is a delimitization, an act of judgment. He was afraid of *beauty* in art or in life because the idea of beauty involves a judgment, an act of definition. He was against boundaries or definitions in life as in art.

This same impetus to destroy definitions is common to the modern and so-called post-modern mind. To define is to discriminate, and discrimination is held to be invariably bad. As a result, many hold homosexuality to be acceptable because it is a denial of moral values or definitions, and godly heterosexuality to be bad because it sees moral boundaries everywhere.

One form of attack on definitions is to redefine words by breaking down some aspects of meaning to extend the boundaries. This is a form of redefinition into obliteration.

This process of altering boundaries has taken place within Christianity. The term "Christian" has been so vaguely defined that its meaning now can include those who deny every doctrine of the Biblical faith.

The same is true of *Christian charity*. Bernard Smith has called attention to the new meanings given to the term. They include political action and armed revolution. It is held to be giving "power to the powerless, political action to change a country's constitution, aid to terrorist groups, and so on."[4]

In the course of such a redefinition, both *Christian* and *charity* are redefined.

According to James 1:27,

> Pure religion and undefiled before God and the Father is this, To visit the fatherless and widows in their affliction, and to keep himself unspotted from the world.

The previous verse in the Greek text ends with the word *religion, threskeia*; in verse 26 true religion and the false are contrasted, and false religion is marked by an unbridled tongue, among other things. But what is "pure religion and unde-

---

4. Bernard Smith, "Christian Aid: The Politics of Charity," in *Conservative Review*, Vol. 1, No. 1, February, 1990, 21-23.

filed"? The modern attitude isolates texts from the context of the whole revelation of God, of which James was familiar. We thus *cannot* honestly limit this definition of religion to visiting orphans and widows in their affliction. The whole range of charitable activities required by God's law are in mind. Similarly, we cannot honestly believe in revelation and isolate the meaning of "pure religion" to caring for widows and orphans. All of biblical theology is presupposed: these words are written to church members who professed to be true believers. They lived close to the resurrection, and the full splendor of that mighty event was close and real to them.

The statement concludes with the words, that one must "keep himself unspotted from the world." Pure religion thus involves all the theological and moral premises of the faith and their outcome in helping meet the needs of those whom God sees as test cases of our faithfulness.

Therefore, we have dealt with humanistic redefinitions of the faith. Such revisionism exists also in evangelical and reformed church circles as well. It is not uncommon for such persons to bridle at James 1:27 and to accuse those who use it of advocating "legalism" or a "works religion." This again is a misuse of Scripture because it isolates a text from the total context of the Bible.

Charity is an important part of the law, the prophets, the psalms, the gospels, and the epistles. It is in fact a distinguishing aspect of Christian faith. Our Lord is very emphatic in declaring "by their fruits ye shall know them" (Matt. 7:20). James, in the verses which immediately follow James 1:27, cites "respect of persons" as at least evidence of evil and blasphemy (James 2:1–10). Then he makes very clear that our actions do test our faith (James 2:11–26). The devils in hell know that there is a God, and they tremble, but they are not saved by their knowledge of that fact (James 2:19). "For as the body without the spirit is dead, so faith without works is dead" (James 2:26). James then goes on to cite sins of the tongue, of speech, as evidence of poor faith (James 3:1–18).

Too many churchmen have assumed that, because the state has a welfare program, they are absolved from the need to do anything in this sphere. It is strange that the early church, living within the Roman Empire, with its very comprehensive welfare system, which included housing and entertainment, "bread and circuses," did not say that the Biblical mandate for charity could be disregarded! Instead, they began, although they were few in number, a major movement, headed by deacons, to meet human needs, *beginning* in their own circles. They obviously did not see, as against our modern churchmen, statist welfare as pleasing to God.

Something is seriously wrong when churchmen see Christian charity as a deformation rather than a reformation. It is heartening to see some local churches returning to the Biblical mandate concerning pure religion.

Christianity is more than a faith. It is the Kingdom of God, ruled by a king, Jesus Christ. It has a law given by God. It has a government, of which all believers are members, citizens, and servants. It requires us to occupy all things until He comes. To restrict the scope of the Kingdom to the inner life is to reduce it to a pagan mystery religion. To curtail the relevancy of the whole law-word of God to salvation is to undermine the meaning of salvation.

Christian charity is a necessary step towards the restoration of Christianity.

THIRTY-ONE

ALMSGIVING

The early church was very much concerned with charity, or almsgiving, as it was for centuries called. The church fathers of that era can be faulted for an inadequate grasp of Biblical theology; they were too much influenced by Greek thinking to be clear-cut on many points. However, what did strongly influence them was the Old and New Testament insistence on charity. Clement's "Second Letter to the Corinthians" was in reality an anonymous sermon, dating from c. 150 A.D. After referring to the Last Judgment, the sermon says,

> Charity, then, like repentance from sin, is a good thing. But fasting is better than prayer, and charity than both. "Love covers a multitude of sins" (Prov. 10:12; 1 Peter 4:8), and prayer, arising from a good conscience, "rescues from death" (James 5:20). Blessed is everyone who abounds in these things, for charity lightens sin.[1]

1. Clement's Second Letter, 16, 4, Cyril C. Richardson, with E. R. Fairweather, E. R. Hardy, M. H. Shepherd, *Early Christian Fathers* (New York, NY: Macmillan, 1970), 200.

The theology of this statement can be faulted; the presuppositions of too many in the early church, including Jews, were Greek. Their application of the faith, however, was Hebraic. They saw the stress throughout the Old Testament, and in the earliest circulating parts of the New Testament canon, on the application of the faith. The result was a dedication to charity that continued into the medieval and Reformation era churches. Scholars, being intellectuals, have tended to stress the theological and philosophical currents more than the practical and charitable applications of the faith.

The kind of practice stressed by John Calvin and St. Charles Borromeo is clearly derived from the early church. In "The First Apology of Justin, the Martyr," we read:

> Chap. LXVII ... And the wealthy among us help the needy; and we always keep together; and for all things wherewith we are supplied, we bless the Maker of all through His Son Jesus Christ, and through the Holy Ghost. And on the day called Sunday, all who live in cities or in the country gather together to one place, and the memoirs of the apostles or the writings of the prophets are read, as long as time permits; then, when the reader has ceased, the president verbally instructs, and exhorts to the imitation of these good things. Then we all rise together and pray, and, as we before said, when our prayer is ended, bread and wine and water are brought, and the president in like manner offers prayers and thanksgivings, according to his ability, and the people assent, saying Amen; and there is a distribution to each, and a participation of that over which thanks have been given, and to those who are absent a portion is sent by the deacons. And they who are well to do, and willing, give what each thinks fit; and what is collected is deposited with the president, who succors the orphans and widows, and those who, through sickness or any other cause, are in want, and those who are in bonds, and the stranger sojourning among us, and in a word takes care of all who are in need. But Sunday is the day on which we all hold our common assembly, because it is the first day on which God's having wrought a change in the darkness and mat-

> ter, made the world; and Jesus Christ our Saviour on the same day rose from the dead.[2]

The weekly services were thus marked by *weekly* offerings to enable the deacons to meet the needs of peoples, and this weekly offering was strongly promoted, we have reason to believe. *Charity was thus an essential part of worship.*

The "Letter of Polycarp to the Philippians" was written before 155 or 156 A.D., when Polycarp was martyred. It counseled men "to walk in the commandments of God." Wives were "to walk in the faith," to love their husbands and to "train up their children in the knowledge and fear of God." Then follows an amazing statement:

> Teach the widows to be discreet as respects the faith of the Lord, praying continually for all, being far from all slandering, evil-speaking, false-witnessing, love of money, and every kind of evil; knowing that they are the altar of God, that He clearly perceives all things, and that nothing is hid from Him, neither reasonings, nor reflections, nor any one of the secret things of the heart.[3]

Godly behavior is required of the widows because "they are the altar of God." An altar is primarily a place of sacrifice, then also a place of prayer. For widows to be called God's *altar* (in some manuscripts, *altars*) is not explained for us. The use is obviously metaphoric, but this does not diminish its importance. It is the widows, Polycarp states, who should know that they are God's altar. Paul, in speaking of widows in Christ's service, calls them "desolate" (1 Tim. 5:5, meaning "alone"). Such a one "trusteth in God, and continueth in supplications and prayers night and day." It is in this sense that a holy widow was an altar. (Later on, when a younger woman was admitted to the circle of widows, a fact which Tertullian noted as unusual and extraordinary, in *On the Veiling of Virgins*, Chapter 9, it was a departure from apostolic practice.) Apart from her prac-

---

2. "The First Apology of Justin Martyr," in Alexander Roberts, James Donaldson, editors, *The Ante-Nicene Fathers*, Vol. 1 (Grand Rapids, MI: Eerdmans, [1867] 1981 reprint), 185f. See also Richardson, *op. cit.*, 287.

3. Donaldson, Roberts, F. Crombie, *op. cit.*, 71.

tical duties (1 Tim. 5:3–16), the widow had a duty to pray for the Christian community. Polycarp, speaking of the presbyters, required, among other things, their oversight of those who had gone astray, of widows generally, of orphans, and the poor.[4] Ignatius, in writing to Polycarp, stressed the care of widows, and he also said, "Do not treat slaves and slave girls contemptuously. Neither must they grow insolent." Caution should be exercised before freeing slaves at the community's expense.[5] The goal of the Christian community was Christ's world dominion, and Polycarp cited 1 Corinthians 6:2, "Do we not know that the saints will judge the world?"[6]

Ignatius held that a church required a bishop, presbyters, and *deacons.* "You cannot have a church without these."[7] Christians had to be a community, not simply a congregation. These offices were the same as the Old Testament offices of prophets and teachers.[8]

There was thus a self-conscious continuity with the Old Testament. The church, with its origin in the twelve disciples replacing the twelve tribes of Israel, was self-consciously "the Israel of God" (Gal. 6:16). The fact that "a great company of priests were obedient to the faith" (Acts 6:7) makes all the more obvious why the Old Testament emphasis on community and charity was so central to the early church: it was Jewish in "membership" to a great degree, and clearly so in character. Faithfulness to the faith of the fathers was very much in evidence, a practical, working faith. We cannot understand the early church except in terms of its Old Testament origin and inheritance.

How important the diaconate was we see in Ignatius' reference to it as "the ministry of Jesus Christ" and to the deacons

4. Richardson, *op. cit.*, Sect. 6, 133.
5. Ibid., "Letter of Ignatius to Polycarp," Sec. 4, 119.
6. Ibid., "Letter of Polycarp to the Philippians, 11:2, 3, 135.
7. Ibid.," Letter of Ignatius to the Trallians," 2:1–2; 99.
8. Ibid., "The Didache," 15:1–2; 178.

"most dear to me."[9] Deacons are therefore to be honored.[10] Hermas said to Christians,

> Give to all, for God wishes His gifts to be shared amongst all. They who receive, will render an account to God why and for what they have received. For the afflicted who receive will not be condemned, but they who receive on false pretences will suffer punishment.[11]

These handfuls of Christians believed that indeed Paul spoke from God when he declared that the saints would judge or rule the world (1 Cor. 6:2). It was therefore held by so simple a pastor as Hermas that sadness of heart and a lack of patience are morally wrong.[12]

Almsgiving is morally right. The word *alms*, from the Greek *eleos*, compassionate, appears in the New Testament, especially in the Sermon on the Mount (Matt. 6:1–4), and also in Luke 11:41; 12:33; Acts 3:2; 3:10; 10:2, 4, 31; and 24:17, also Acts 9:36. The word is singular although it has a plural form. *Alms* means *charity*, but it also conveys the meaning, as Patrick Fairbairn pointed out, of active pity, of compassion that leads to practical help. For this reason, it is at times spoken of as almsdeeds (Acts 9:36). In this latter text, Dorcas is described as "full of good works and almsdeeds which she did." In the late nineteenth century, Fairbairn observed,

> In the present state of evangelical Christendom, especially in the existing condition of its large towns, it may well be doubted whether there is enough of living Christianity in its churches and of co-operative love, to enable them adequately to undertake the oversight of the poor, if such a charge were to be devolved upon them.[13]

---

9. "Ignatius, To the Magnesians," Chap. 6, in Roberts, Donaldson and Crombie, *The Writings of the Apostolic Fathers*, 177).

10. "Ignatius, To the Trallians," Chap. 3; Ibid., 191-92.

11. Ibid., "The Pastor of Hermas," Commandment Second, 350.

12. Ibid., "Commandment Fifth," 356-57.

13. Patrick Fairbairn, "Alms," in Patrick Fairbairn *The Imperial Bible Dictionary*, Vol. 1 (Grand Rapids: MI: Zondervan, n.d., reprint of 1891 edition), 131-134.

Worse yet, to many people, almsgiving smacks of medievalism and Rome, although they would find it difficult to condemn, given the fact that the reformers were strongly in favor of it.

The first century A. D. saw the extremes of the concept of *love.* For the Roman poet, Ovid, it meant basically sexual technique. For the New Testament community, love meant the grace of God received and passed on to others in practical help: it means community.[14]

The Roman Catholic position has been that "The obligation of almsgiving is complementary to the right of property." From early days, the malicious, the intemperate, and the lazy were excluded by apostolic requirements.[15] Private ownership of property is a privilege given to men by God, Who is the owner of all things, for "the earth is the LORD's, and the fullness thereof; the world and they that dwell therein" (Ps. 24:1). *All things* are God's property, including mankind. Our possession of the earth is as stewards thereof, totally responsible to God for our use of the earth and of one another. Hence the medieval view that with property there went an obligation of almsgiving was thoroughly Biblical. The modern view of a purely private "right" to property is humanistic and anti-Biblical.

Leviticus 25:35–38 is important in that *redemption* is given as an additional reason for charity:

> 35. And if thy brother be waxen poor, and fallen in decay with thee; then thou shalt relieve him: yea, though he be a stranger, or a sojourner; that he may live with thee.
> 36. Take thou no usury of him, or increase: but fear thy God; that thy brother may live with thee.
> 37. Thou shalt not give him thy money upon usury, nor lend him thy victuals for increase.

---

14. William Klassen, "Love, NT and Early Jewish Literature," in David Noel Freedman, *The Anchor Bible Dictionary*, Vol. 4, K-N (New York, NY: Doubleday, 1992), 381-396.

15. James David O'Neill, "Alms," in *The Catholic Encyclopedia*, Vol. 1 (New York, NY: The Encyclopedia Press, [1907] 1913), 328-331.

> 38. I am the LORD your God, which brought you forth out of the land of Egypt, to give you the land of Canaan, and to be your God.

Psalm 24 tells us that God owns us; we are His property and His stewards. Leviticus 25:35–38, *first,* declares that God commands as our Redeemer, the Redeemer of Israel from its sin and Egypt (and of us, from our bondage to sin). *Second,* our charity is to extend, not only to fellow-believers, but to strangers or aliens. *Third,* where charity is required, no money can be given on interest if the help needed is a loan. Because the Lord is our Creator and Redeemer, *all* the conditions of life are governed by His law-word. He being our Creator alone can be our Lawgiver. To reject His law in any sphere, including charity, is to reject Him, whatever we may profess otherwise.

How closely related charity is to true faith we see in Job 29:12–17:

> 12. … I delivered the poor that cried, and the fatherless, and him that had none to help him.
> 13. The blessing of him that was ready to perish came upon me: and I caused the widow's heart to sing for joy.
> 14. I put on righteousness, and it clothed me: my judgment was as a robe and a diadem.
> 15. I was eyes to the blind, and feet was I to the lame.
> 16. I was a father to the poor: and the cause which I knew not I searched out.
> 17. And I brake the jaws of the wicked, and plucked the spoil out of his teeth.

There is much more of this in Job, as witness 31:5–40. Clearly, in all the Bible charity is a test of true faith.

Our Lord is also emphatic here, as witness Luke 14:12–14, words that make clear how far we are from Old and New Testament *requirements*:

> 12. Then said he also to him that bade him, When thou makest a dinner or a supper, call nor thy friends, not thy brethren, neither thy kinsmen, nor thy rich neighbours;

> lest they also bid then again, and a recompense be made thee.
> 13. But when thou makest a feast, call the poor, the maimed, the lame, the blind:
> 14. And thou shalt be blessed; for they cannot recompense thee; for thou shalt be recompensed at the resurrection of the just.

Clearly, our Lord was a disturber of the peace. Paul reminds believers that our Lord had said, "It is more blessed to give than to receive" (Acts 20:35). In Galatians 2:10, Paul tells us that the leaders in Jerusalem welcomed him and Barnabas as commissioned to go "unto the heathen" (2:9), "Only they would that we should remember the poor; the same which I also was forward to do." The word *forward* can be rendered as *eager.*

A key test which for centuries governed Christian charity was Matthew 25:40, "And the King shall answer and say unto them, Verily I say unto you, Inasmuch as ye have done it unto one of the least of these my brethren, ye have done it unto me." We see this stressed in various ways. In a twelfth century book cover made for the psalter of Queen Melisende of the Latin Kingdom of Jerusalem, we see a king, perhaps her husband Fulk, feeding the hungry, giving them something to drink, clothing the naked, comforting the sick, welcoming the stranger, and visiting prisoners.[16]

In 1460, in Rome Cardinal Torrecremata founded the Confraternity of the Annunciation, to provide dowries for poor girls. By the beginning of the twentieth century, it was still doing so, although a double amount was by then given to girls entering religious orders.

All this only skims the surface. It is important to remember that at one time Christians, through a variety of organizations, confraternities, foundations, and orders provided for health, education, charity, the arts, and more, while the state limited itself to warfare and justice. In the 1990s, after a lecture in one

---

16. Geoffrey Barraclough, editor, *The Christian World* (New York: NY: Harry R. Abrams, Publishers, 1981), 124.

state, a legislator commented privately about observations made in a closed committee meeting. All recognized that the state's financial survival was being threatened by welfarism. It was actually stated, with *unofficial* assent, that perhaps welfare recipients should be parceled to all the churches, with a summons to resume their historic role of charity. Most churches would be shocked if told that this was once their duty under the Lord. They read the Bible with a veil over their eyes.

Scripture Index

Index

The Author

Rousas John Rushdoony (1916-2001) was a well-known American scholar, writer, and author of over thirty books. He held B.A. and M.A. degrees from the University of California and received his theological training at the Pacific School of Religion. An ordained minister, he worked as a missionary among Paiute and Shoshone Indians as well as a pastor to two California churches. He founded the Chalcedon Foundation, an educational organization devoted to research, publishing, and cogent communication of a distinctively Christian scholarship to the world-at-large. His writing in the *Chalcedon Report* and his numerous books spawned a generation of believers active in reconstructing the world to the glory of Jesus Christ. Until his death, he resided in Vallecito, California, where he engaged in research, lecturing, and assisting others in developing programs to put the Christian Faith into action.

The Ministry of Chalcedon

CHALCEDON (kal-see-don) is a Christian educational organization devoted exclusively to research, publishing, and cogent communication of a distinctively Christian scholarship to the world at large. It makes available a variety of services and programs, all geared to the needs of interested ministers, scholars, and laymen who understand the propositions that Jesus Christ speaks to the mind as well as the heart, and that His claims extend beyond the narrow confines of the various institutional churches. We exist in order to support the efforts of all orthodox denominations and churches. Chalcedon derives its name from the great ecclesiastical Council of Chalcedon (AD 451), which produced the crucial Christological definition: "Therefore, following the holy Fathers, we all with one accord teach men to acknowledge one and the same Son, our Lord Jesus Christ, at once complete in Godhead and complete in manhood, truly God and truly man...." This formula directly challenges every false claim of divinity by any human institution: state, church, cult, school, or human assembly. Christ alone is both God and man, the unique link between heaven and earth. All human power is therefore derivative: Christ alone can announce that, "All power is given unto me in heaven and in earth" (Matthew 28:18). Historically, the Chalcedonian creed is therefore the foundation of Western liberty, for it sets limits on all authoritarian human institutions by acknowledging the validity of the claims of the One who is the source of true human freedom (Galatians 5:1).

The Chalcedon Foundation publishes books under its own name and that of Ross House Books. It produces a magazine, *Faith for All of Life*, and a newsletter, The *Chalcedon Report*, both bimonthly. All gifts to Chalcedon are tax deductible. For complimentary trial subscriptions, or information on other book titles, please contact:

Chalcedon
Box 158
Vallecito, CA 95251 USA
(209) 736-4365
www.chalcedon.edu